SEW
BEAUTIFUL

MAKE STYLISH HANDMADE CLOTHING WITH SIMPLE STITCH-AND-WEAR PATTERNS

KENNIS WONG

CREATOR OF ITCH TO STITCH

PAGE STREET
PUBLISHING CO.

DEDICATION

TO MY AA BAAK

PAGE STREET
PUBLISHING CO.

First published in 2020 by

Page Street Publishing Co.

27 Congress Street, Suite 105

Salem, MA 01970

www.pagestreetpublishing.com

Distributed by Macmillan, sales in Canada by The Canadian Manda Group.

24   23   22   21   20   1   2   3   4   5

ISBN-13: 978-1-64567-136-7

ISBN-10: 1-64567-136-4

Library of Congress Control Number: 2019957233

Cover and book design by Laura Benton for Page Street Publishing Co.

Photography by Ray Morgan

Printed and bound in China

CONTENTS

INTRODUCTION

Sewing has always been my refuge. I feel powerful creating something beautiful that I am proud of. It is such a pleasure to transform a piece of fabric into a one-of-a-kind garment. I'd be lying, however, if I told you sewing is always puppies and rainbows. True, for the most part, the sewing process is therapeutic, but at times it can be frustrating, even for me. However, the most important thing is that I always feel a great sense of satisfaction overcoming the challenges. When I hold a finished garment in my hands, I feel like I can conquer the world! Then I am ready for the next beautiful challenge. Yes, sewing is very addicting too.

I started sewing when I was thirteen years old. Neither my mom nor grandma knew how to sew, at least not more than hemming or mending by hand, but fortunately, my school required us to take a sewing class. Even though the class was mandatory, I didn't feel like learning to sew was a chore. In fact, it was one of the most enjoyable classes I've ever taken. I have forgotten many details, but I remember that my first garment was a baby dress. I also have a fond memory of going to the fabric store with my classmates to choose a fabric. The classroom was mostly equipped with Singer treadle sewing machines, and that was what I used to sew the baby dress. I was hooked immediately. If this were a movie, I would have vowed to become a designer or a seamstress at that point. But no, I didn't. I only knew that I liked it. I was passionate enough to keep sewing beyond the school sewing classes, but I had no idea that sewing would become such a big part of my life.

After a while, I learned to make sewing patterns. Initially, patternmaking was my way to understand fit. One thing led to another, and I began making sewing patterns for other women too. In 2014, I started Itch to Stitch Designs, where I offer digital sewing patterns to sewing hobbyists. My focus is on modern yet elegant styles for advanced beginners and beyond. I am proud to say that my loyal customers love Itch to Stitch for its well-drafted patterns, clever techniques and thorough instructions.

The designs of Itch to Stitch center on wearability. As much as I appreciate the beauty of a complicated special-occasion dress, I spend my time wearing casual and work-appropriate clothing that suits my lifestyle. I would like to spend my time making that type of clothing, aiming to have a complete and functional self-sewn wardrobe. I make sewing patterns for like-minded people.

You will find the designs in this book to be simple, elegant and wearable. You will be able to wear your beautiful garments to have coffee with friends in a café, walk your dog in the park, run errands around town, go on a date with your sweetheart and cheer your kids on at their next game. There is no need to wait until the next fancy party to wear these clothes!

If you have sewn a very simple garment or home decor item before, then you will be able to sew the patterns in this book. The detailed instructions and illustrations will walk you through creating the garments step by step. The difficulty of the designs increases gradually throughout the book, so you will gain confidence and sewing skill as you work on each design.

I know you will enjoy *Sew Beautiful*. You are going to be so proud of yourself for making and wearing your very own custom-made clothes!

Kennis Wong

FUNDAMENTALS FOR YOUR SEW BEAUTIFUL PROJECTS

Before starting your sewing project, I encourage you to read through this section. Those of you with a few sewing projects under your belt may learn some new approaches or sewing tips that make sewing easier. To those newer to sewing, don't worry if you don't remember everything after you've read it once. The projects will refer to this chapter when a new technique is used.

This information is not meant to be an exhaustive list of sewing tools and techniques—very far from it, in fact. It is meant only to support the sewing projects in this book. Also, there are different ways to achieve the same result. For the sake of simplicity, I go over the method that I typically use or the method that I think is appropriate for someone who is less experienced in sewing.

TOOLS

ESSENTIAL

Besides the fabric recommended for each project, here are the tools you should have before you begin:

1. **SEWING MACHINE**—Your sewing machine should be capable of making a straight stitch (forward and reverse) and a zigzag stitch. No other fancy stitches will be necessary.

2. **SEWING MACHINE NEEDLES**—You'll use universal machine needles when sewing woven garments and jersey (ballpoint) or stretch machine needles when sewing knit garments. It's ideal to use a brand-new needle for each project. For lightweight to medium-weight fabric, a size 80/12 needle is a good choice.

3. **PINS**—You'll need pins to hold the layers of fabric together temporarily before stitching a seam.

4. **MATCHING THREAD**—I use a good-quality 100% polyester sew-all thread. It is strong and does not shrink.

5. **SEAM RIPPER**—Even the most experienced sewing hobbyists make mistakes. You will need a seam ripper to undo the stitches of a seam.

6. **SOFT TAPE MEASURE**—You will need a soft tape measure to measure yourself before choosing a size.

7. **SEAM GAUGE**—The seam gauge is my most-used tool of all. I am constantly using it to measure the accuracy of my seam, hem and markings.

8. **IRON AND IRONING BOARD**—I cannot emphasize enough the importance of pressing to achieve professional results. It is not enough to press after the project is complete; you need to press each seam after you sew it and before you stitch an intersecting seam.

9. **SCISSORS**—Most sewing hobbyists have at least two pairs of scissors, one for cutting fabric and one for cutting the pattern paper.

10. **TRANSLUCENT PAPER AND PENCIL**—The pattern pieces for each design are printed on one page. You will need to trace the outlines and markings for the size you need onto a piece of translucent paper. I use medical exam paper; it is large, easy to see through and economical.

OPTIONAL

Some tools are also nice to have; they make your sewing easier. However, it is possible to start sewing without them.

1. **PINKING SHEARS**—One quick and easy way to minimize fraying of a fabric is to pink the cut edges using a pair of pinking shears.

2. **ERASABLE MARKER**—There are a few options on the market. You can use tailor's chalk or a chalk wheel. A heat-erasable marking pen is also available; test it on a scrap, however, to see if it leaves any marks on your specific type of fabric.

3. **TRACING PAPER AND TRACING WHEEL**—These tools help you transfer the markings from the paper pattern to your fabric.

4. **SEE-THROUGH, STRAIGHT EDGE RULER**—This type of ruler is useful when lengthening or shortening your pattern pieces.

5. **SERGER OR OVERLOCK MACHINE**—A serger, also called an overlock machine, is great for stitching knit fabric. It sews, trims the seam allowances and finishes the edges in one pass; thus, it is a big time-saver. However, a serger is only an optional tool. You can use your regular sewing machine to do the same job.

6. **PRESSING TOOLS**—I love my seam roll and tailor's ham for pressing. They allow me to isolate a seam to press without making an impression in unwanted places. However, they are optional and you can still complete your sewing projects without them.

MEASURING YOURSELF

You will need your bust, waist and hip circumference measurements to find the correct size. The best tools for the job are a soft tape measure and a full-length mirror. Whether you are measuring the bust, waist or hip, place the soft tape measure in one place first. Wrap it around your body tautly but not too tight, and bring the other end in a full circle to meet the starting point. The soft tape measure needs to be parallel to the ground all the way around your body.

BUST

The bust measurement should be taken at the fullest part of the chest. Depending on your shape, this may or may not be at the same level as the nipples. If you are not sure, you can measure at one level first, then move the tape measure up or down an inch (or a couple of centimeters) and measure again. Make sure that when you move the tape measure, the entire circumference is still parallel to the ground. The largest number is where the fullest part of your bust is.

WAIST

The waist measurement should be taken at the narrowest part of the waist. Don't worry about where your belly button is relative to the narrowest part of your waist; it can vary depending on your body shape and height. If you don't have a defined waist and are not sure where the narrowest part is, tie a string snugly around your midsection. Then move your waist left and right until the string settles at one spot. Measure your waist using that spot around your body.

HIP

The hip measurement should be taken at the fullest part of your hip. You may be surprised where the fullest part of your hip is until you start measuring. That is because this measurement includes the buttocks, which might hang high or low. Therefore, I advise you to move your tape up or down (while keeping the tape measure parallel to the ground) until you find the fullest part of your hip.

Each chapter of this book includes instructions on how to pick a size. Even though the body measurements are consistent across all designs, sometimes you may need to disregard the waist or hip measurement because of a design feature. For example, in the Castlepoint Skirt (page 99), you cannot choose a smaller size for the waist, because otherwise you will not be able to pull the skirt up past your hips.

People always ask whether I use American, UK or European sizing. My answer is always none of the above. The reality is that even with two brands that claim to use American sizing, they will likely have different fits due to the popularity of vanity sizing, which is an arbitrary sizing not based on standard measurements. Size labels are nothing more than just labels. Therefore, to get a great fit, you should always compare your actual body measurements to the body measurements for the pattern according to the instructions. Do not use your ready-to-wear sizing to pick a size. Any good sewing pattern will tell you to do the same regardless of the brand.

The finished garment measurements for each design are included for your reference. As you become more experienced in sewing, the finished garment measurements will give you a better idea about the intended fit and the design ease of the garment. Note that the finished garment measurements are for the garments in their non-stretched state. In other words, if you are using a knit fabric for the garment, the finished garment measurements may vary depending on the stretch percentage of your fabric.

It is perfectly fine if you have to use one size for the bust, another size for the waist and another size for the hip. In fact, many women, myself included, have to do just that. See Blending Sizes (page 11) for more details.

Women's figures can fluctuate a lot over time, so I encourage you to measure yourself or the intended recipient right before you sew a new garment. Also, be sure to wear the intended undergarment when you measure yourself. Different undergarments can give you different results!

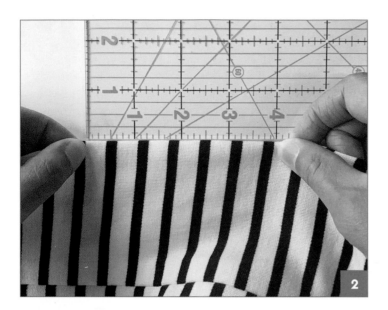

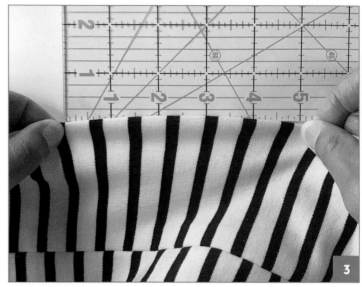

CHOOSING AND PREPARING YOUR FABRIC

Each pattern is designed for a specific type of fabric. On the most basic level, some patterns are designed for knit fabric, while others are for woven fabric. Most of the time, the two types of fabric are not interchangeable unless you make adjustments to the patterns. I suggest that you use the recommended fabric for the patterns in this book.

If you purchase your fabric online, it's typical that the vendor tells you if the fabric is a knit fabric. If the listing doesn't specify, it is usually a woven fabric. If you are purchasing in person and you are unsure of the fabric type, don't be afraid to ask the salesperson.

KNIT FABRIC

Knit fabric is stretchy and you can comfortably make big movements in a garment made with knit fabric. For example, a T-shirt is made with knit fabric. Garments made with knit fabric usually have a casual feel to them. You will notice that when a knit fabric is recommended for a pattern, a stretch percentage is also recommended. This is an important figure. If your knit fabric has less stretch than recommended, your garment will end up too tight. Likewise, if your knit fabric has more stretch than recommended, your garment will be too loose.

Here is how you can determine the stretch percentage.

1. Fold your piece of fabric and put the fold next to a ruler.

2. Measure 4 inches (10 cm) of the fold. You can just hold that amount between your hands. Note that you are not stretching any fabric at all.

3. Stretch the fabric with your right hand, while keeping the left hand stationary. Stretch as much as you can without straining your fabric.

4. Let's say you are able to stretch your fabric from 4 inches to 5 inches (or 10 cm to 12.5 cm). That means the fabric has a 25% stretch. Here's how the math goes: (5-4) / 4 = 25% [or (12.5-10) / 10 = 25%].

You can do the same test on both the horizontal (lengthwise) and vertical (widthwise) directions of the fabric. Most of the time, the requirement only specifies the horizontal stretch percentage, but there are occasions that the vertical stretch requirement is specified too.

If you are purchasing the fabric in person, you can do this test before you purchase the fabric. Unfortunately, fabric vendors online don't always specify this percentage. But do contact them and ask them about it before you make the purchase.

Some online vendors give you the percentage of elastane, spandex or Lycra™ in the fabric. Note that this is not the same as the stretch percentage, and it is not convertible to the stretch percentage.

WOVEN FABRIC

Garments made with woven fabric have more structure. They usually look more formal. Many woven fabrics have no stretch, but to complicate things a little, sometimes spandex or Lycra fiber is added to the woven fabric to give it a little stretch. Also, a woven fabric may have a mechanical stretch, in which the fabric is woven in a way that achieves very minimal give without any stretchy fiber. All of these modern additions to the woven fabric are for making the garments more comfortable to wear, while still maintaining a more structured and formal appearance. The woven pattern designs in this book require non-stretch fabric only. If you decide to use a woven fabric that has some stretch, then the resulting garment will be slightly more relaxed. In that case, you may choose a size smaller to compensate.

PRE-TREAT THE FABRIC

Pre-treat your fabric in the same way that you plan to clean the garment after sewing. If you plan to wash or dry clean your finished garment, you should always wash or dry clean your fabric before cutting it. This way, the fabric will have shrunk before you cut it. The fabric requirements stated in this book assume that your fabric is already pre-shrunk.

PREPARING THE PATTERN PIECES

BLENDING SIZES

You may need to choose different sizes for the bust, waist and hip by blending sizes. See Measuring Yourself (page 9) to pick the correct sizes based on your measurements.

1. At the bottom of the armhole, choose a size that fits your bust. If you are between sizes, choose the larger size if you like your garment more relaxed, otherwise, choose the smaller size. You will use this size for your armhole, neckline and shoulders too.

2. Draw a very gentle curve from one size in the bust to another size in the waist. The waist is usually indicated by a notch at the narrowest point in the midsection.

3. If necessary, draw another gentle curve from one size in the waist to another size in the hip.

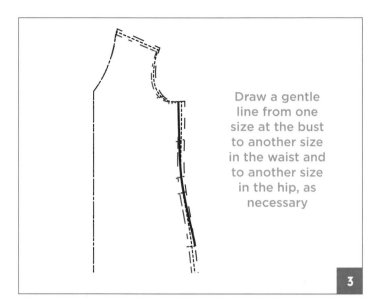

Draw a gentle line from one size at the bust to another size in the waist and to another size in the hip, as necessary

3

LENGTHENING OR SHORTENING

All the patterns in this book are based on the body height of 5 feet 6 inches (168 cm) regardless of the size. However, that doesn't mean you can't use the patterns if you are taller or shorter. In fact, many of my users are 5 feet (152 cm) or 5 feet 10 inches (178 cm). You can lengthen or shorten the sewing patterns using the lengthen or shorten line included in the pattern pieces. Whenever appropriate, you can find these lines on the upper bodice, lower bodice, skirt and/or sleeve pieces.

For my 5-foot-3-inch (160-cm) stature with shorter legs, I regularly shorten ½ inch (1.25 cm) on the upper body and 1½ inches (3.8 cm) on the lower body (pants or skirt). If your body is relatively proportional, you may choose to lengthen or shorten more evenly between the upper and lower body. This may take some experience, but once you figure out your adjustments, the same amount should apply across all patterns.

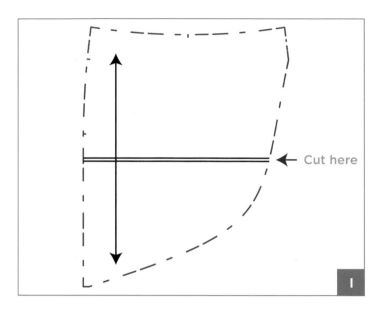

Cut here

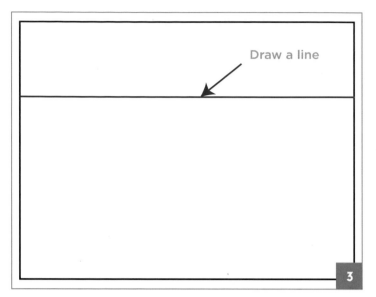

Draw a line

TO LENGTHEN

1. Cut the pattern apart at the lengthen or shorten line.

2. Use a piece of blank paper that is large enough to accommodate the width of the pattern piece and the amount that you plan to add lengthwise.

3. Draw a horizontal line at the upper end of the paper.

4. Tape the upper part of the pattern piece to the paper, with the lengthen or shorten line aligned to the horizontal line.

5. Note that in all cases, the grainline is included on the pattern piece and is perpendicular to and intersects the lengthen or shorten line.

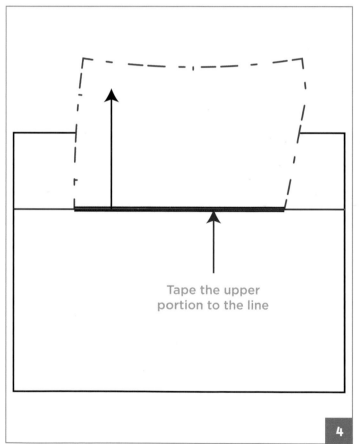

Tape the upper portion to the line

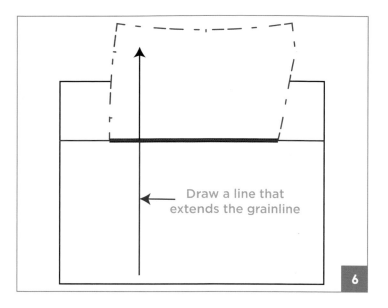

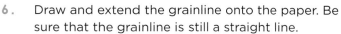

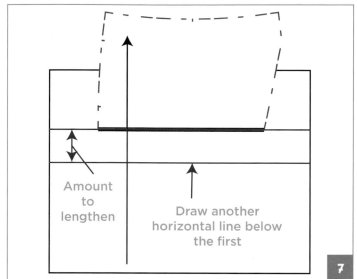

6. Draw and extend the grainline onto the paper. Be sure that the grainline is still a straight line.

7. Draw another line below and parallel to the first horizontal line. The gap in between is the amount you want to lengthen.

8. Tape the lower part of the pattern piece to the paper, with the lengthen or shorten line aligned to the second horizontal line. Make sure that the grainline on the pattern piece is aligned to the grainline extension.

9. Draw a line to connect the upper and lower portions. Sometimes this is a straight line, but most of the time it is not. You will need to draw a gradual line to connect the two and to ensure the transition is smooth. To do so, it might be necessary to remove or add a little to the original line to ensure a smooth transaction.

10. Cut out the pattern piece using the new lines.

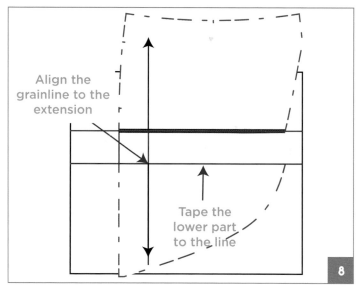

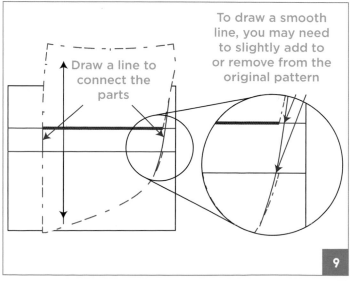

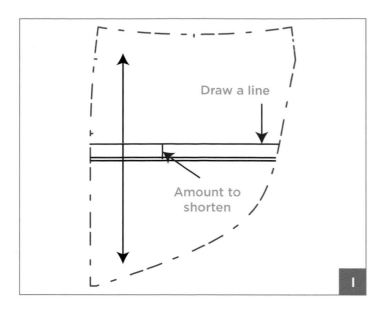

Draw a line

Amount to shorten

1

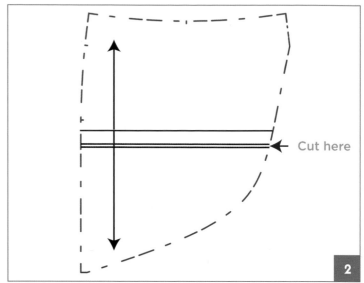

Cut here

2

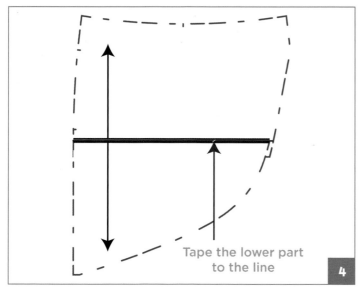

Tape the lower part to the line

4

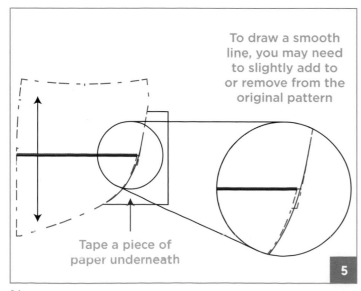

To draw a smooth line, you may need to slightly add to or remove from the original pattern

Tape a piece of paper underneath

5

TO SHORTEN

1. On the pattern piece, draw a line that is above and parallel to the lengthen or shorten line. The gap in between should be the amount you plan to shorten.

2. Cut the pattern apart at the lengthen or shorten line.

3. Note that in all cases, the grainline is included on the pattern piece and is perpendicular to and intersects the lengthen or shorten line.

4. Tape the lower part of the pattern piece to the upper part of the pattern piece, with the lengthen or shorten line aligned to the line you drew. Make sure the grainline on the pattern piece is still connected.

5. If there is a jog at the edge of the pattern pieces, tape a small piece of paper underneath. You will need to draw a gradual line to connect to eliminate the jog. It might be necessary to remove or add a little to the original line to ensure a smooth transition.

6. If there is any marking on the pattern piece that is covered (you can see better if you hold the pattern pieces up to the light), redraw the marking.

7. Cut out the pattern piece using the new lines.

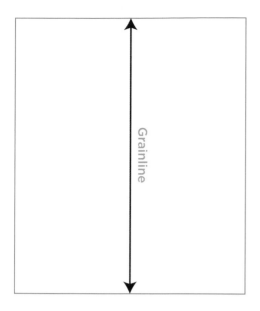

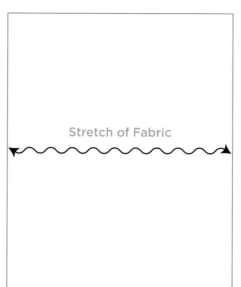

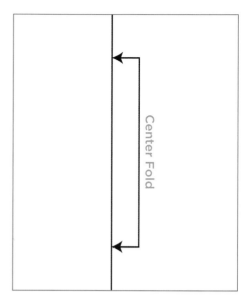

PATTERN NOTATIONS

A few notations are on the pattern pieces to assist your cutting and sewing of the fabric.

GRAINLINE

To ensure that the garment hangs properly on your body, you have to respect the grainline when cutting out the pattern pieces from the fabric. The notation of the grainline is a straight line with an arrow on each end. When you place the pattern piece on the fabric, the grainline should be parallel to the selvage of the fabric. The selvage is the self-finished edge of the fabric where the fabric doesn't ravel. You will also see tiny holes left during manufacturing along the selvage.

STRETCH OF FABRIC

In patterns designed for knit fabric, I include the Stretch of Fabric marking. It means that you should orient the fabric so that the stretchiest part follows that direction. For the patterns in this book, the Stretch of Fabric marking is always perpendicular to the grainline.

NUMBER OF PIECES TO CUT

The pattern specifies the number of pieces you need to cut out. You may see "Cut 2 Mirror Images of Primary Fabric." That means you need to cut out two pieces of primary fabric using that pattern piece, and those two pieces need to be mirror images—usually one for the left and one for the right side of your body. The easiest way to cut out two mirror images is to cut the pattern piece on a folded or double layer of fabric.

CENTER FOLD

Some pattern pieces must be cut on the fold. That means you need to fold the fabric lengthwise first. This fold should be parallel to the selvage. Place the pattern piece with the marked straight edge against the fold. You will end up with a single piece of fabric with its left and right side a mirror image of each other.

The fold usually indicates the center front or center back. To mark the center front or center back, I make a ⅛-inch (3-mm) snip using my scissors at the top and bottom edges of the fold. Note that you never make any snip in the middle of the fold, or you would make a hole in the fabric.

NOTCH

The markings you see most are notches. They are there to help you align two pieces of fabric correctly. Conventionally, single notches are placed on the front and sides, whereas double notches are placed on the back. When there is a concentration of notches, I sometimes place a letter next to a notch so I can accurately refer to it in the process.

Note that notches are always placed at the edge of the fabric. In my case, I like to make a little snip into the seam allowance with my scissors to mark my notch. The snips are not long, about ⅛ inch (3 mm). You can also mark with chalk or an erasable marker if the fabric frays easily and a snip might not be visible.

CIRCLE OR CROSS

In addition to using notches to match up the pieces, I also use circles or crosses for alignment. Each project's instructions will always explain what to do with the circle or cross. Also, I sometimes add a label (such as "front" or "back") next to the circle or cross if there is potential for confusion.

STABILIZATION

Stabilization is important to provide an internal structure where necessary. You will see two types of stabilization in the patterns in this book: interfacing and stay tape.

INTERFACING

Interfacing is applied on the wrong side of the fabric to make it stiffer. The garment will also last longer with interfacing. In this book, only some of the garments designed for woven fabric will use interfacing; therefore, we will only use fusible woven or weft insertion interfacing. Woven interfacing is designed for woven fabric, whereas weft insertion interfacing can be used on both woven and knit fabrics. Fusible interfacing has little heat-activated glue dots on one side, so it will stick to the wrong side of the fabric when you press the interfacing with your iron. Different manufacturers have different methods for applying the interfacing, so make sure you read their instructions. Also, some fusible interfacing will require pre-shrinking. I prefer to use the kind that does not require pre-shrinking so I don't have to soak and hang the interfacing to dry before using it.

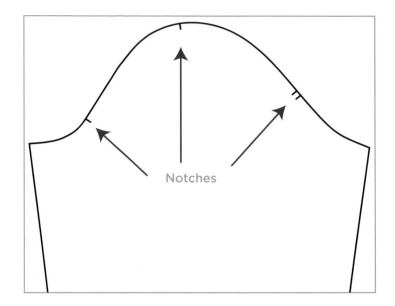

Notches

STAY TAPE

In a few garments, I need to restrict the stretch of the fabric at the shoulders and neckline. Although there are different ways to achieve the same goal, my preferred way is to use fusible stay tape. Fusible stay tape is really just fusible interfacing in a strip form. Just like interfacing, fusible stay tape has little heat-activated glue dots on one side, so it will stick to the wrong side of the fabric when you press the interfacing with your iron. You should be able to buy it as a roll in ½-inch (1.25-cm) or ⅜-inch (1-cm) width. You may see straight fusible stay tape or bias fusible stay tape. For our purpose, we will use straight fusible stay tape. If you cannot find any, it is perfectly acceptable to make your own using fusible interfacing. You only have to cut strips in the desired width from your interfacing. Just be sure they are cut on the straight grain, which means the length of the strip should be parallel to the selvage of the interfacing.

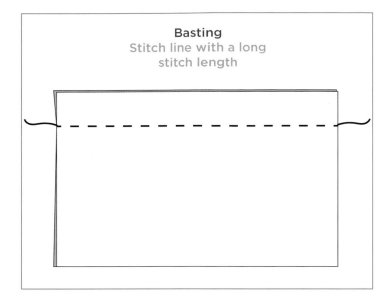

Basting
Stitch line with a long
stitch length

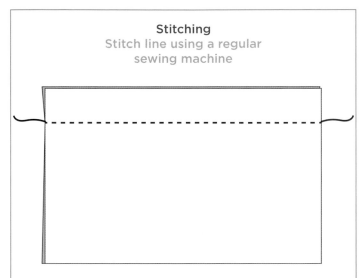

Stitching
Stitch line using a regular
sewing machine

PUTTING YOUR GARMENT TOGETHER

BASTING

Basting is a stitch to temporarily hold layers of fabric together. You use a long stitch length—for example, 4.5 mm—to sew a straight line through the layers. With the long stitch length, the stitches are easier to remove later. Some people choose not to remove the basting if it is not visible on the right side of the final garment. Other times, it is necessary to remove the basting. For example, in the Palermo Blouse and Tiered Dress (page 115), the center front is basted together, but the stitches need to be removed later to create the split neckline. To remove a line of basting, use your seam ripper to break and pull out the thread.

STITCHING AND SERGING

For woven garments, you will sew the seams with a regular sewing machine using a straight stitch. For knit garments, you have the choice to sew the seam with a serger. A serger trims the seam allowances, sews the seam and finishes the edge in one pass, so it is much faster than using your sewing machine. When a seam is serged, the seam remains stretchy. The instructions will specify "stitch," which means to use a sewing machine, or "serge," which means to use a serger if you have one.

If you don't have a serger, don't worry. You can always use a regular sewing machine. When using a regular sewing machine to stitch knit fabric, I recommend that you use a narrow zigzag stitch so that the seams will stretch slightly. I use a stitch that is 2.5 mm long and 0.5 mm wide. You will barely notice the width of the zigzags.

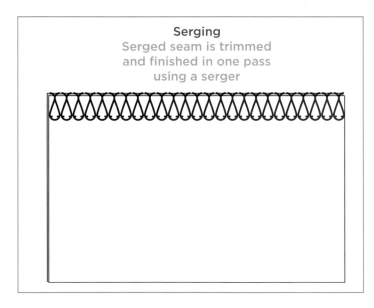

Serging
Serged seam is trimmed
and finished in one pass
using a serger

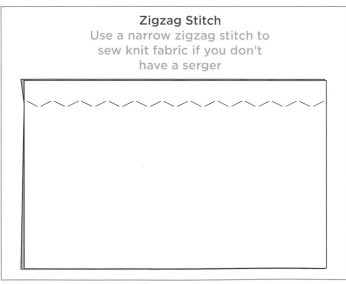

Zigzag Stitch
Use a narrow zigzag stitch to
sew knit fabric if you don't
have a serger

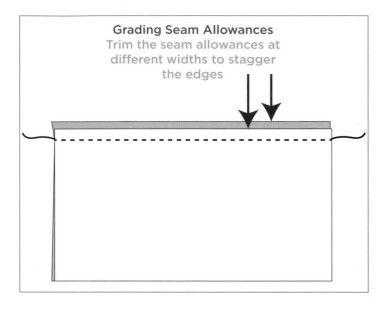

Grading Seam Allowances
Trim the seam allowances at different widths to stagger the edges

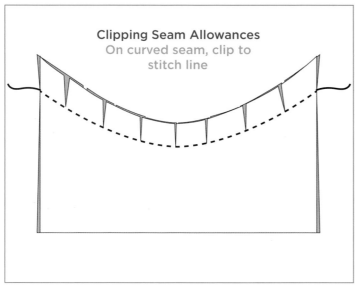

Clipping Seam Allowances
On curved seam, clip to stitch line

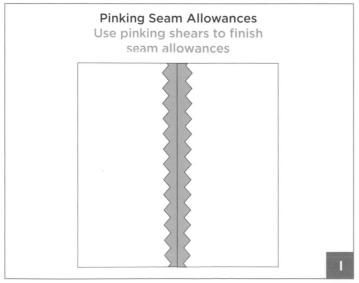

Pinking Seam Allowances
Use pinking shears to finish seam allowances

SEAM ALLOWANCES

The included seam allowance is ½ inch (1.25 cm) for woven garments and ⅜ inch (1 cm) for knit garments.

GRADING SEAM ALLOWANCES

Grading a seam allowance is a good way to reduce bulk at a seam. It also helps reduce the impression of the seam allowance shown on the right side of the garment. Usually you grade the seam allowances when they are pressed to one side (as opposed to pressing them open). You might also want to grade if there are more than two layers of fabric in a seam, regardless of which way you press the seam allowances. To grade, use your scissors to trim one of the seam allowances shorter, hence staggering the edges of the seam allowances. The general rule of thumb is to trim shorter the seam allowance that is closest to the body in the final garment. There is no hard rule for how much of the seam allowances to trim. For thinner fabric, I trim half of one seam allowance. For example, if the seam allowance is ½ inch (1.25 cm) wide, I trim ¼ inch (6 mm) of it. I leave the other seam allowance untrimmed. For a thicker fabric, I trim ⅜ inch (1 cm) on one seam allowance and trim ¼ inch (6 mm) on the other seam allowance. If there are more than two layers, you just trim the first one the most and the last one the least. As long as the seam allowances stagger, you are doing it correctly.

CLIPPING SEAM ALLOWANCES

When you are sewing a curved seam, you need to clip the seam allowances so they lay flat and smooth when the fabric is turned right side out. To clip a seam, use your scissors to make a small cut from the edge to the seam line. Take care not to cut through the seam line. The curvier the seam, the closer the clips should be. At the curvy part of a neckline, I clip the seam allowances every ¼ inch (6 mm) or so. Clip each seam allowance separately and stagger the cuts so that the seam is not weakened too much in one spot.

FINISHING SEAM ALLOWANCES

You can choose to finish the raw edges in different ways. The purpose of finishing is to prevent the raw edges from fraying. This is done mostly on the raw edges of the seam allowances, but the technique is also used for facings and the raw edges of a hem.

For woven fabric, you can:

1. Pink the edges with pinking shears.

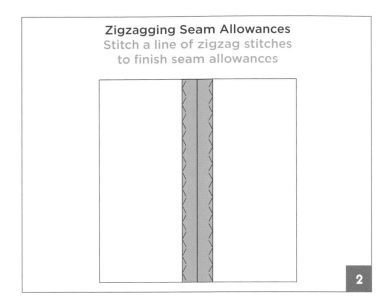

Zigzagging Seam Allowances
Stitch a line of zigzag stitches
to finish seam allowances

2

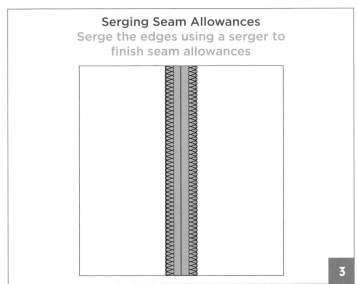

Serging Seam Allowances
Serge the edges using a serger to
finish seam allowances

3

2. Stitch a line of zigzag stitches along the edges.

3. Serge the edges with a three-thread overlock stitch using a serger—a four-thread overlock stitch is also acceptable, although it is slightly bulkier than the three-thread counterpart.

There are certainly a dozen more ways to finish the seam allowances on your woven garments, but for the projects in this book, I encourage you to go simple. You can get fancier as you gain more experience.

For knit fabric, you can use your serger to serge, trim and finish the edges in a single pass using the four-thread stitch. That means you won't have to separately finish the edges of the seam allowances. If you choose to stitch your knit garment using a regular sewing machine, finishing the seam allowance edges may not be necessary because many knit fabrics don't fray. In case you are working with a knit fabric that does fray, you can choose to stitch a line of zigzag stitches along the edges.

UNDERSTITCHING

Understitching is a technique in which you sew the seam allowances to the lining or facing. The effect of this technique is that the seam will slightly roll toward the lining or facing. This is particularly useful for a neckline or a sleeveless armhole. To understitch, press the seam allowances toward the lining or facing, then sew a line of straight stitches through all layers (two or more seam allowances and the lining or facing) ⅛ inch (3 mm) from the seam line. If you are also grading, clipping or finishing the seam allowances, do them first before understitching.

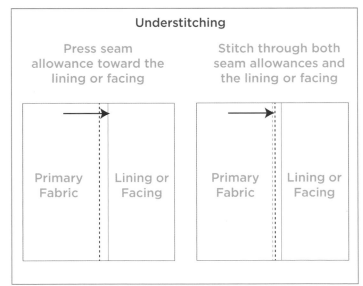

Understitching

Press seam allowance toward the lining or facing

Stitch through both seam allowances and the lining or facing

| Primary Fabric | Lining or Facing | Primary Fabric | Lining or Facing |

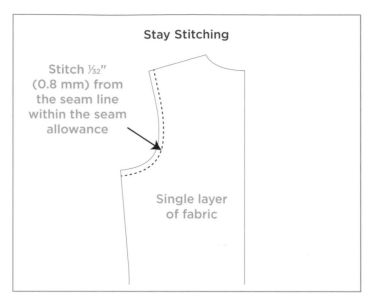

Stay Stitching

Stitch 1/32" (0.8 mm) from the seam line within the seam allowance

Single layer of fabric

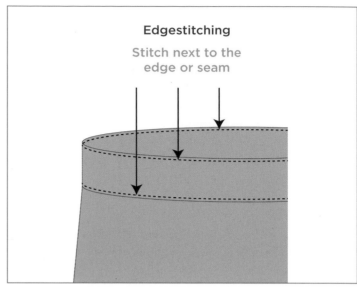

Edgestitching

Stitch next to the edge or seam

Topstitching

A line of straight stitching anywhere on the garment

Stitching in the Ditch

Stitch on an existing seam

Stitch through the back layer

STAY STITCHING

The purpose of stay stitching is to keep a certain part of a garment from stretching out of shape during handling and wearing. Stay stitching is a regular line of straight stitching done on a single layer of fabric within the seam allowance, ideally 1/32 inch (0.8 mm) from the seam line. Stay stitching is also useful when you plan to clip the seam allowance for any reason. The line of stay stitching prevents the fabric from ripping beyond the stitch line. Stay stitching, however, is not a substitute for fusible stay tape. There is still a tiny bit of stretch in a line of stay stitching, and fusible stay tape can prevent that stretch better than stay stitching.

EDGESTITCHING

An edgestitch is a regular line of straight stitching done next to an edge, a seam or a fold. It is usually about 1/16 inch (1.6 mm) from the edge, seam or fold. While the stitch is mostly decorative, it can help to hold the seam allowance down and to reduce some seam bulk.

TOPSTITCHING

A topstitch is essentially the same as an edgestitch except it is done anywhere on the garment other than along the edge. Topstitching is mostly decorative, but at times it is used to stitch a pocket onto a garment.

STITCHING IN THE DITCH

Stitching in the ditch means that you stitch directly in the seam. When done accurately, the stitch line will be hidden from view. Usually there is another layer of fabric behind the seam, so while stitching in the ditch, you are stitching through that back layer. This technique is used in various parts of a garment, but most notably done in the waistband.

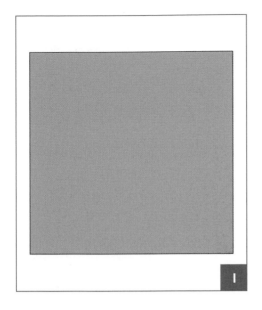

1

2

3

INSTRUCTION NOTATION

1. Right side of primary fabric
2. Wrong side of primary fabric
3. Right side of lining
4. Wrong side of lining
5. Right side of contrast fabric
6. Wrong side of contrast fabric
7. Interfacing or stay tape

4

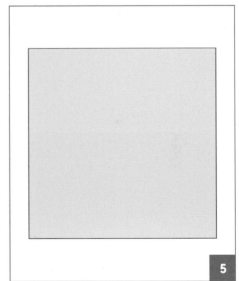

5

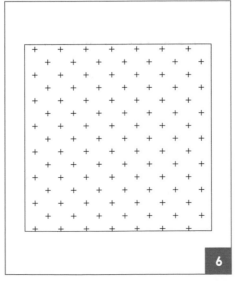

6

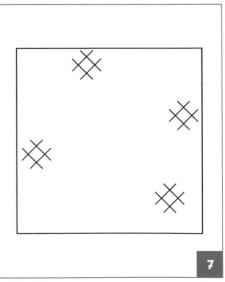

7

SEW YOUR BEAUTIFUL WARDROBE

Sew Beautiful includes eight flattering designs with eighteen variations. Half of them are patterns for knit fabric and the other half are for woven fabric. I believe that a modern and well-rounded wardrobe should have pieces from both types of fabric, and sewing with both is a good skill to hone. These projects cater to people who are newer to sewing; someone who has completed a few simple clothing projects in the past should be able to tackle these projects with relative ease.

With years of supporting sewing hobbyists, I understand that some people can be intimidated by zippers or button closures. I specifically came up with designs without these elements. I present the projects in order of difficulty, so you can start from the beginning and gain confidence as you work your way through the book. This progressive approach doesn't mean that these patterns are not for sewing veterans. If you have years of sewing experience, you will still appreciate these understated and tasteful designs, as well as the instant gratification that comes with quick projects.

I love to name my patterns after places because I love traveling. I have visited some of these places, but a couple are still on my wish list. If you are not familiar with these places, I encourage you to look them up. Perhaps by learning about them, you can also experience my feeling when I designed these patterns.

THE MORNINGTON

The Mornington is a relaxed-fit woven garment with a V neck and an A-line silhouette. I think the Mornington is elegant simplicity at its finest. While looking chic, the Mornington is also roomy and comfortable. The waist is defined by the adjustable waist tie.

In addition to a sleeveless top option, the Mornington also comes in a sleeveless dress option and a dress with flare sleeves option. The hem of the dress reaches the knee, while the top option is at hip length. For all options, the bodice is completely lined.

I think the flare sleeves add a certain drama and feminine flair to the Mornington, but if you prefer, the instructions walk you through making a sleeveless version too.

SLEEVELESS TOP
(SEE PHOTO ON PAGE 6)

FRONT   BACK

SLEEVELESS DRESS
(SEE PHOTO ON PAGE 24)

FRONT   BACK

DRESS WITH FLARE SLEEVES
(SEE PHOTO ON PAGE 22)

FRONT   BACK

CHOOSING YOUR SIZE

1. Compare your bust circumference (the fullest part of your measured bust) to the "Body Measurements" table. Choose the size that best fits your bust. If your measurement is between sizes, choose the smaller size if you like your garment more fitted; otherwise, choose the bigger size.

2. Compare your hip circumference (the fullest part of your measured hip) to the "Body Measurements" table. Choose the size that best fits your hips. If your measurement is between sizes, choose the smaller size if you like your garment more fitted; otherwise, choose the bigger size.

3. If you have different sizes for the bust and hip, you can blend sizes (page 11). The waist is designed to be very relaxed, and you do not have to blend sizes to accommodate the waist when selecting a size.

MATERIALS

PRIMARY FABRIC
Use a very lightweight to lightweight woven fabric with no stretch. Lawn cotton, chambray, crepe and linen are good choices.

LINING
Use a very lightweight woven fabric with no stretch. Batiste and voile are good choices. If your primary fabric is very lightweight, you can also use the same fabric.

OTHER MATERIALS
76 inches (193 cm) of ⅜-inch (1-cm)- or ½-inch (1.25-cm)-wide straight fusible stay tape (page 16); you can also cut your own using lightweight woven fusible interfacing on the straight grain.

BODY MEASUREMENTS

	SIZE	00	0	2	4	6	8	10	12	14	16	18	20
BUST	(IN)	31⅛	32½	33⅞	35⅛	36½	37⅞	39¼	40⅝	42	43¼	44⅝	46
	(CM)	79	82.5	86	89	92.5	96	99.5	103	106.5	110	113.5	117
HIP	(IN)	33¼	34⅝	35⅞	37¼	38⅝	40	41¼	42⅝	44	45⅜	46⅝	48
	(CM)	84.5	88	91	94.5	98	101.5	105	108	112	115	118.5	122

FINISHED GARMENT MEASUREMENTS

	SIZE	00	0	2	4	6	8	10	12	14	16	18	20
BUST	(IN)	34⅜	35¾	37¼	38⅝	40⅛	41½	43	44⅜	45⅞	47¼	48¾	50¼
	(CM)	87	91	94.5	98	102	105.5	109	113	116.5	120	124	127.5
WAIST	(IN)	32½	34	35⅜	36⅞	38¼	39¾	41¼	42⅝	44⅛	45½	47	48⅜
	(CM)	82.5	86	90	93.5	97.5	101	105	108.5	112	115.5	119.5	123
HIP	(IN)	36⅝	38⅛	39½	41	42½	43⅞	45⅜	46⅞	48¼	49¾	51¼	52⅝
	(CM)	93	97	100.5	104	108	111.5	115	119	122.5	126.5	130	133.5

FABRIC REQUIREMENTS

PRIMARY FABRIC (54 INCHES/137 CM WIDE)													
		00	0	2	4	6	8	10	12	14	16	18	20
SLEEVELESS TOP	(YARD)	1⅜	1⅜	1⅜	1⅜	1⅜	1⅜	1½	1½	1½	1⅞	1⅞	1⅞
	(CM)	125	125	125	125	125	125	135	135	135	170	170	170
SLEEVELESS DRESS	(YARD)	1⅝	1⅝	1⅝	1⅞	1⅞	1⅞	2½	2½	2½	2½	2½	2½
	(CM)	150	150	150	170	170	170	230	230	230	230	230	230
DRESS WITH FLARE SLEEVES	(YARD)	2	2	2	2¼	2¼	2¼	2⅞	2⅞	2⅞	3	3	3
	(CM)	190	190	190	205	205	205	260	260	260	275	275	275
LINING (54 INCHES/137 CM WIDE)													
		00	0	2	4	6	8	10	12	14	16	18	20
SLEEVELESS TOP	(YARD)	⅞	⅞	⅞	⅞	⅞	⅞	1⅛	1⅛	1⅛	1½	1½	1½
	(CM)	80	80	80	80	80	80	100	100	100	135	135	135
BOTH DRESS OPTIONS	(YARD)	1⅛	1⅛	1⅛	1⅜	1⅜	1⅜	2⅛	2⅛	2⅛	2⅛	2⅛	2⅛
	(CM)	105	105	105	125	125	125	195	195	195	195	195	195

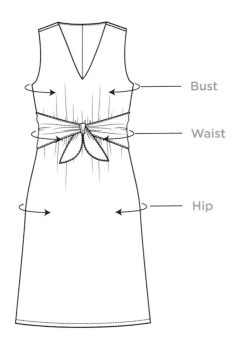

Bust

Waist

Hip

FABRIC CUTTING INSTRUCTIONS

PATTERN PIECE	FROM PRIMARY FABRIC, CUT	FROM LINING, CUT
1 - Front	1 on fold*	1 on fold**
2 - Back	2 mirror images*	2 mirror images**
3 - Sleeve (for the Dress with Flare Sleeves only)	2 mirror images	0
4 - Waist Tie	2 sets of 2 mirror images	0

*Use the hem marked "Cut Here for the Primary Fabric for the Sleeveless Top Option" or "Cut Here for the Primary Fabric for the Sleeveless Dress or Dress with Flare Sleeves Option" accordingly.
**Use the short hem marked "Cut Here for the Lining for the Sleeveless Top Option" or "Cut Here for the Lining for the Sleeveless Dress or Dress with Flare Sleeves Option" accordingly.

LAYOUT DIAGRAMS
SLEEVELESS TOP (PRIMARY FABRIC)

SIZES OO TO 8

Selvage

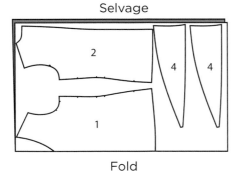

Fold

SIZES IO TO I4

Selvage

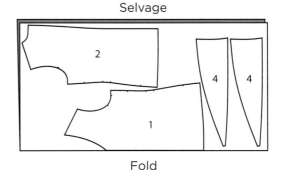

Fold

SIZES I6 TO 20

Selvage

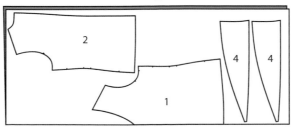

Fold

(CONTINUED)

LAYOUT DIAGRAMS

SLEEVELESS DRESS (PRIMARY FABRIC)

SIZES OO TO 2

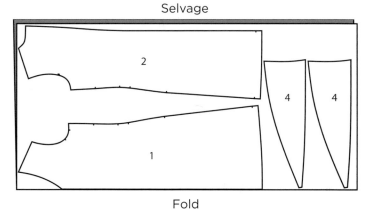

SIZES 4 TO 14

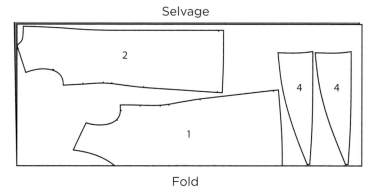

SIZES 16 TO 20

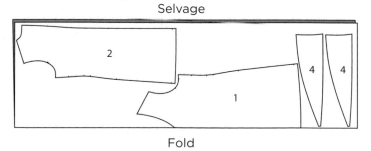

DRESS WITH FLARE SLEEVES (PRIMARY FABRIC)

SIZES OO TO 2

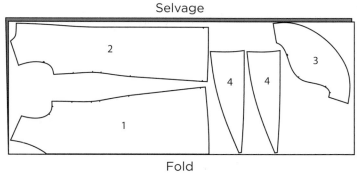

SIZES 4 TO 14

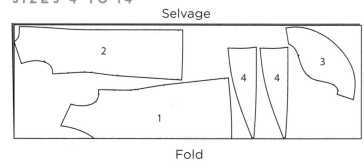

SIZES 16 TO 20

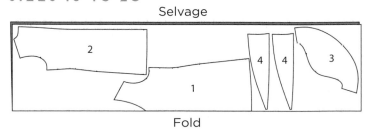

SLEEVELESS TOP (LINING)

SIZES 00 TO 8

Selvage

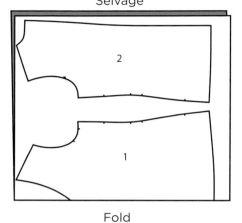

Fold

SIZES 10 TO 14

Selvage

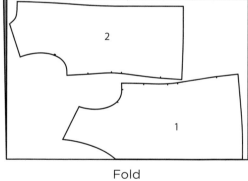

Fold

SIZES 16 TO 20

Selvage

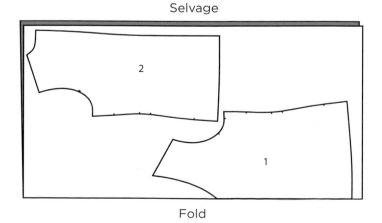

Fold

SLEEVELESS DRESS OR DRESS WITH FLARE SLEEVES (LINING)

SIZES 00 TO 2

Selvage

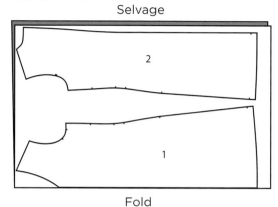

Fold

SIZES 4 TO 14

Selvage

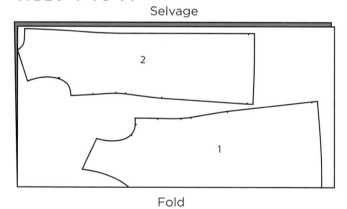

Fold

SIZES 16 TO 20

Selvage

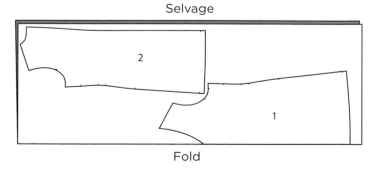

Fold

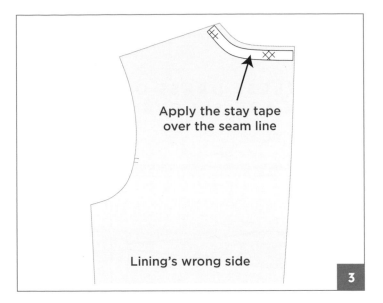

Apply the stay tape over the seam line

Lining's wrong side

3

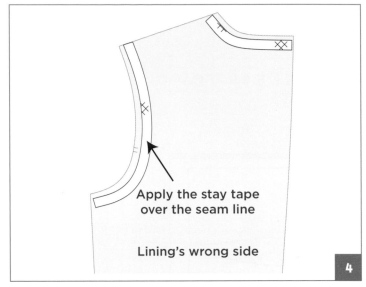

Apply the stay tape over the seam line

Lining's wrong side

4

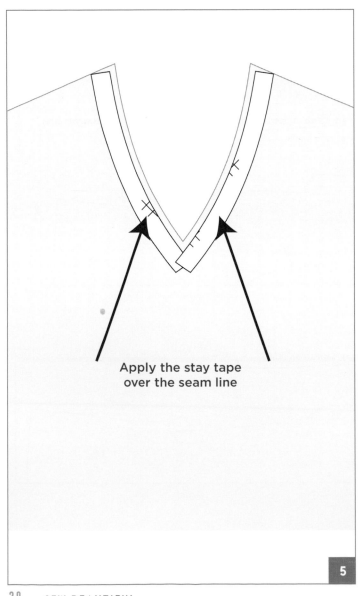

Apply the stay tape over the seam line

5

SEAM ALLOWANCES

The included seam allowances are ½ inch (1.25 cm) unless stated otherwise in the process.

PROCESS

The same method is used for both the top option and the dress option. The top option is used for the illustrations.

CUTTING AND MARKING FABRIC

1. Trace the pattern outlines for your size and option onto a piece of paper (see back envelope), then cut the fabric according to the Layout Diagrams (pages 27–29).

2. Transfer all the markings to the fabric before removing the pattern pieces (pages 15–16).

Follow steps 3 to 27 for the Sleeveless Top or Sleeveless Dress. Skip to step 28 for the Dress with Flare Sleeves.

STABILIZATION

3. On the wrong side of the Back (2) lining, using a hot iron, apply the stay tape onto the back neckline, centered over the seam line. The seam line is ½ inch (1.25 cm) from the cut edge. Repeat for the other Back lining piece.

4. On the same Back lining, apply the stay tape onto the back armhole, centered over the seam line as well. Repeat for the other Back lining piece.

5. On the wrong side of the Front (1) lining, apply the stay tape onto the front neckline, centered over the seam lines on both sides of the V neckline. The seam line is ½ inch (1.25 cm) from the cut edge.

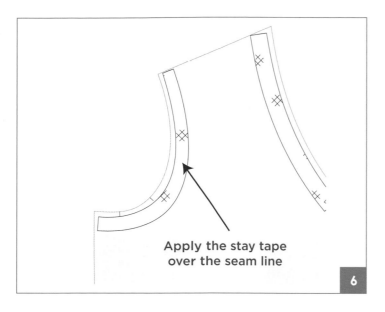

Apply the stay tape
over the seam line

6

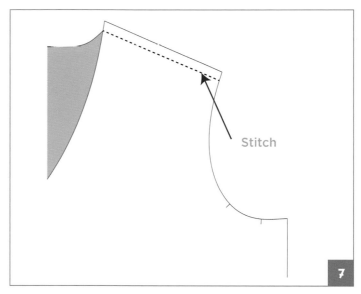

Stitch

7

6. On the same Front lining, apply the stay tape onto the front armhole, centered over the seam line as well.

SHOULDER

7. Using the primary fabric, with the right sides together, pin the Front to the Back at the shoulder. Stitch. Using a hot iron, press the seam allowances open. Finish the seam allowances as desired (page 18). Repeat for the other shoulder. We will refer to this assembled piece as the primary fabric Bodice below.

8. Repeat step 7 for the Front and Back lining pieces as well. We will refer to this assembled piece as the lining Bodice below.

NECKLINE

9. With the right sides together, pin the lining Bodice to the primary fabric Bodice at the neckline. Stitch from the center back edge to the point of the Front. Putting the needle down in the fabric and without cutting the thread, turn and continue to stitch to the other edge of the Back.

10. Grade the seam allowances (page 18) with the seam allowances of the lining trimmed shorter.

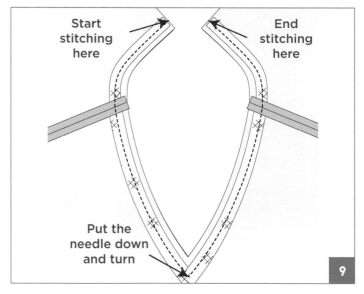

Start stitching here

End stitching here

Put the needle down and turn

9

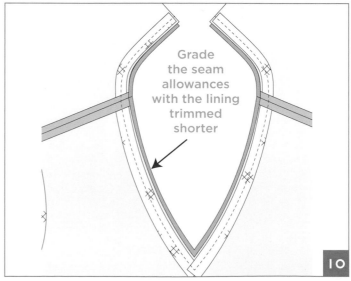

Grade the seam allowances with the lining trimmed shorter

10

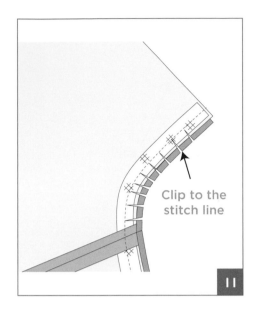

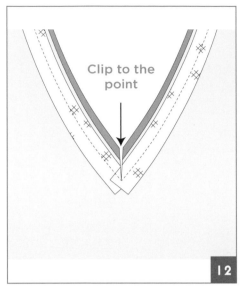

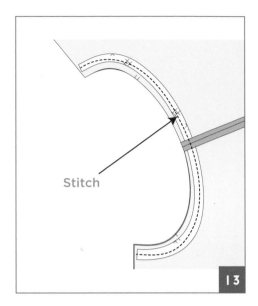

Clip to the stitch line

Clip to the point

Stitch

11

12

13

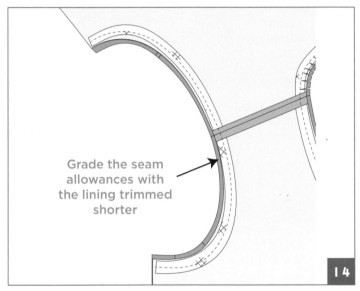

Grade the seam allowances with the lining trimmed shorter

14

11. Along the back neckline, using your scissors, clip to the stitch line (page 18) every ¼ inch (6 mm) or so. Take care not to clip beyond the stitch line.

12. Using your scissors, clip to the point of the V at the front neckline.

ARMHOLE

13. With the right sides together, pin the lining Bodice to the primary fabric Bodice at the armhole. Stitch.

14. Grade the seam allowances with the seam allowances of the lining trimmed shorter.

15. Along the armhole, using your scissors, clip to the stitch line every ¼ inch (6 mm) or so. Take care not to clip beyond the stitch line. Repeat steps 13 to 15 for the other armhole.

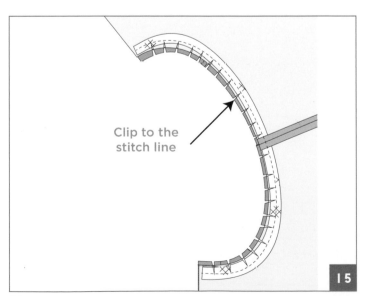

Clip to the stitch line

15

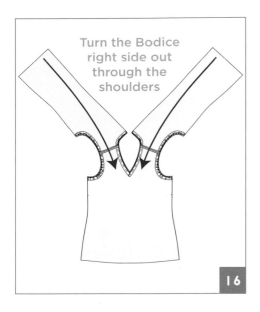

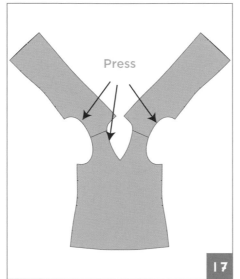

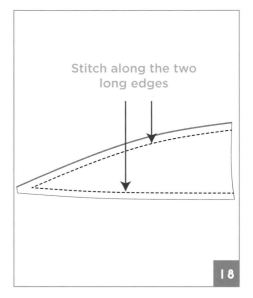

16. Turn the Bodice right side out by pulling the Back pieces through the shoulders.

17. Press the armholes and neckline with the seams slightly rolled to the lining side.

WAIST TIE

18. With the right sides together, pin two pieces of the Waist Tie (4) together. Stitch along the two long edges. Trim the seam allowances to ⅛ inch (3 mm) wide.

19. Turn the Waist Tie right side out.

20. Edgestitch (page 20) close to the seams.

21. Repeat steps 18 to 20 for the remaining two Waist Tie pieces.

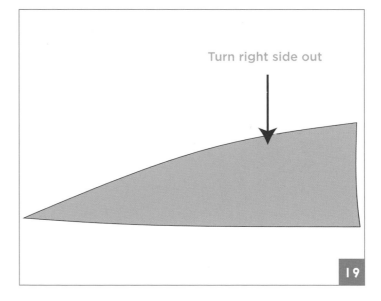

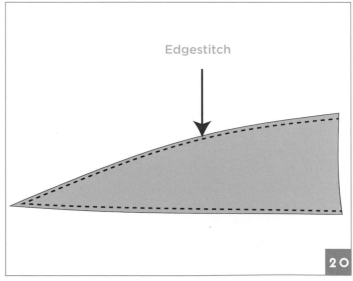

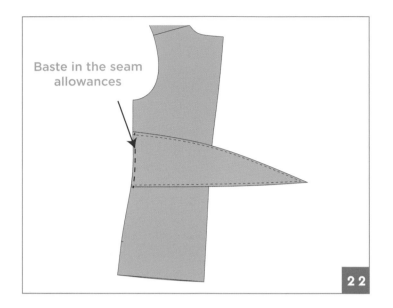

Baste in the seam allowances

22

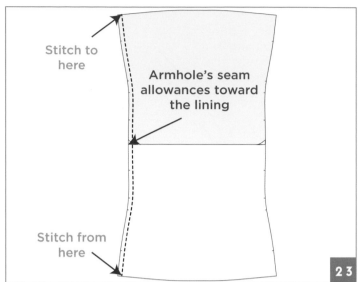

Stitch to here

Armhole's seam allowances toward the lining

Stitch from here

23

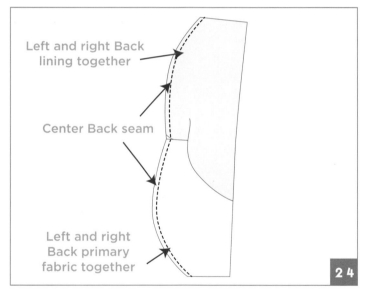

Left and right Back lining together

Center Back seam

Left and right Back primary fabric together

24

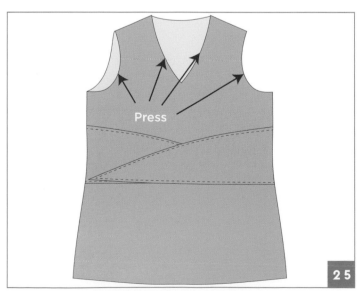

Press

25

22. With the lining out of the way, pin the assembled Waist Tie to the right side of the Back primary fabric at the waist, matching the notches. Orient the Waist Tie so that the top edge of the Waist Tie marked A matches the notch marked A on the Back. Baste (page 17) in the seam allowances. Repeat for the other Waist Tie.

SIDE AND BACK

23. Open up the Bodice to separate the primary fabric from the lining. With the right sides of the Front lining and Back lining together and the right sides of the Front primary fabric and Back primary fabric together, pin the side seam. Arrange the seam allowances of the armhole so that they are pointing toward the lining. Stitch the side seam in one continuous line. Press the seam allowances open. Finish the seam allowances as desired. Repeat for the other side.

24. Similar to the previous step, with the Bodice open, pin the left and right Back lining together and pin the left and right Back primary fabric together at the center back seam. Stitch the back seam in one continuous line. Press the seam allowances open. Finish the seam allowances as desired.

25. Turn the Bodice right side out and press.

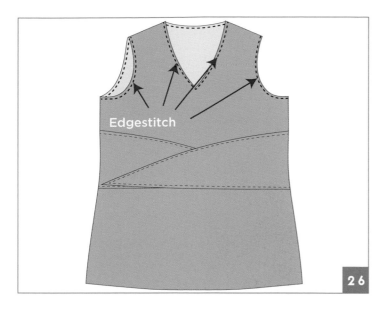

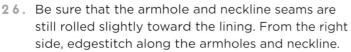

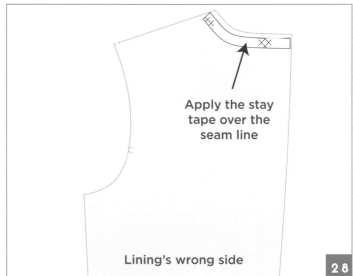

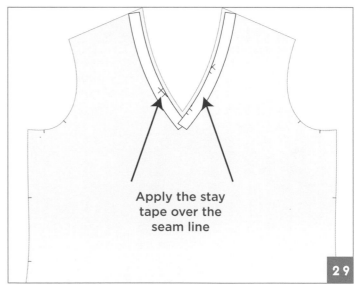

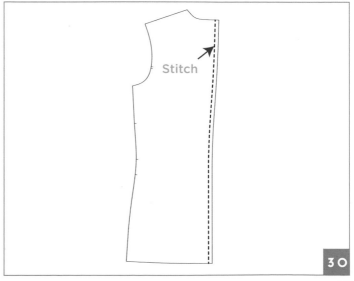

26. Be sure that the armhole and neckline seams are still rolled slightly toward the lining. From the right side, edgestitch along the armholes and neckline.

27. Skip to step 50 to finish the Sleeveless Top or Sleeveless Dress.

Follow steps 28 to 52 for the Dress with Flare Sleeves.

STABILIZATION

28. On the wrong side of the Back (2) lining, using a hot iron, apply the stay tape onto the back neckline, centered over the seam line. The seam line is ½ inch (1.25 cm) from the cut edge. Repeat for the other Back lining piece.

29. On the wrong side of the Front (1) lining, apply the stay tape onto the front neckline, centered over the seam lines on both sides of the V neckline. The seam line is ½ inch (1.25 cm) from the cut edge.

BACK

30. With the right sides together, pin the two Back primary fabric pieces together at the center back. Stitch. Press the seam allowances open. Finish the seam allowances as desired (page 18).

31. Repeat step 30 for the two Back lining pieces as well.

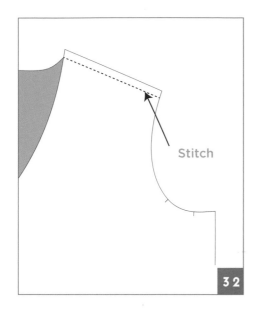

Stitch

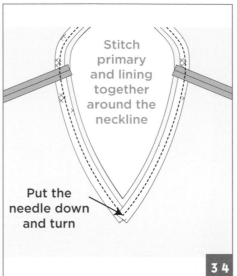

Stitch primary and lining together around the neckline

Put the needle down and turn

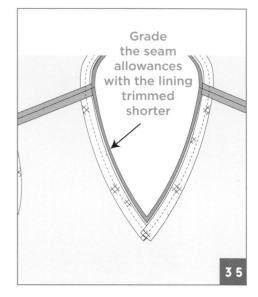

Grade the seam allowances with the lining trimmed shorter

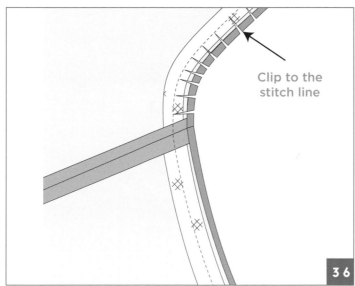

Clip to the stitch line

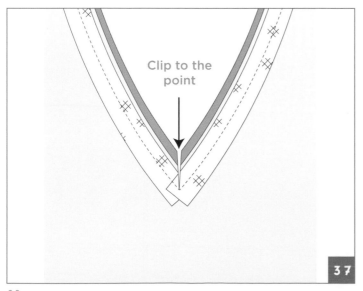

Clip to the point

SHOULDER

32. Using the primary fabric, with the right sides together, pin the Front to the Back at the shoulder. Stitch. Using a hot iron, press the seam allowances open. Finish the seam allowances as desired. Repeat for the other shoulder.

33. Repeat step 32 for the shoulders of the Front and Back lining pieces as well.

NECKLINE

34. With the right sides together, pin the lining Bodice to the primary fabric Bodice at the neckline. Stitch from the center back to the point of the Front. Putting the needle down in the fabric and without cutting the thread, turn and continue to stitch to the other side of the center back.

35. Grade the seam allowances (page 18) with the seam allowances of the lining trimmed shorter.

36. Along the back neckline, using your scissors, clip to the stitch line (page 18) every ¼ inch (6 mm) or so. Take care not to clip beyond the stitch line.

37. Using your scissors, clip to the point of the V at the front neckline.

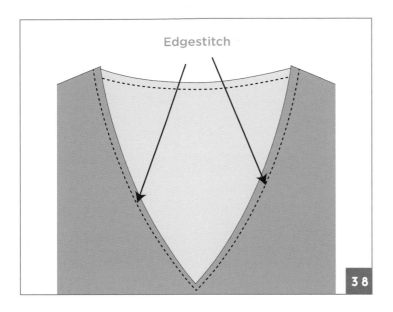

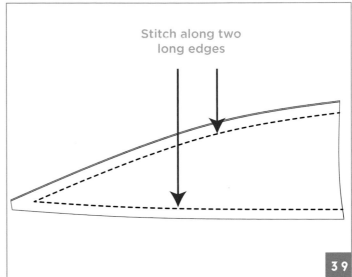

38. Turn the Bodice right side out and press. Be sure that the neckline seam is rolled slightly toward the lining. From the right side, edgestitch (page 20) along the neckline.

WAIST TIE

39. With the right sides together, pin two pieces of the Waist Tie (4) together. Stitch along the two long edges. Trim the seam allowances to ⅛ inch (3 mm) wide.

40. Turn the Waist Tie right side out.

41. Edgestitch close to the seams.

42. Repeat steps 39 to 41 for the remaining two Waist Tie pieces.

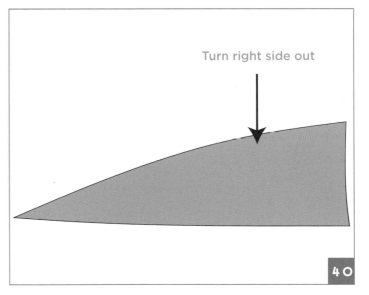

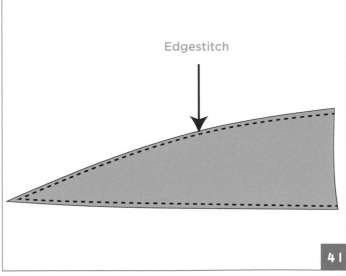

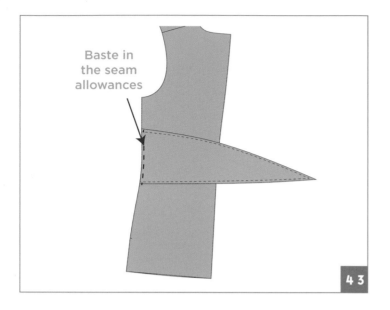

Baste in the seam allowances

43

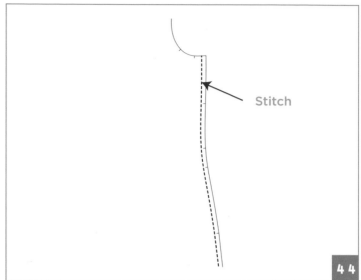

Stitch

44

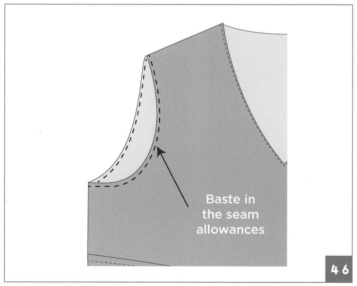

Baste in the seam allowances

46

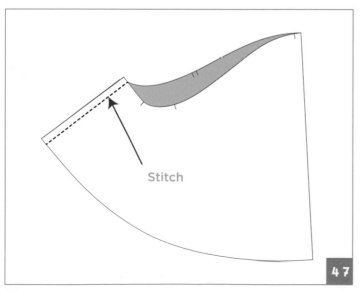

Stitch

47

4 3 . Pin the assembled Waist Tie to the right side of the Back primary fabric at the waist, matching the notches. Orient the Waist Tie so that the top edge of the Waist Tie marked A matches the notch marked A on the Back. Baste (page 17) in the seam allowances. Repeat for the other Waist Tie.

SIDE

4 4 . Using the primary fabrics, with the right sides together, pin the Front to the Back at the side, making sure that the lining is out of the way. Stitch. Press the seam allowances open. Press the seam allowances of the Waist Tie toward the Back. Finish the seam allowances as desired. Repeat for the other side. We will refer to this assembled piece as the primary fabric Bodice below.

4 5 . Repeat step 44 for the Front and Back lining pieces as well. We will refer to this assembled piece as the lining Bodice below.

SLEEVE

4 6 . Turn the Bodice right side out. Baste the primary fabric Bodice and lining Bodice together at the armhole within the seam allowances. The two layers will be treated as one piece in the following steps. Repeat for the other armhole.

4 7 . With the right sides together, stitch the seam of the Sleeve (3). Press the seam allowances open. Finish the seam allowances as desired. Repeat for the other Sleeve.

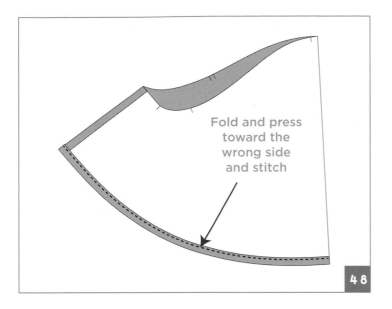

Fold and press toward the wrong side and stitch

48

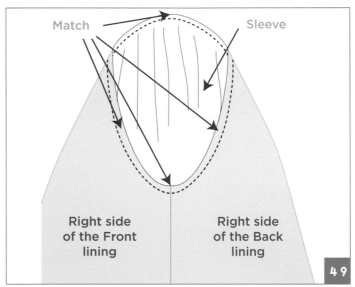

Match   Sleeve

Right side of the Front lining

Right side of the Back lining

49

48. Fold and press ½ inch (1.25 cm) of the hem of the Sleeve toward the wrong side twice. Edgestitch close to the first fold. Repeat for the other Sleeve.

49. With the right sides of the primary fabric together, place the Sleeve inside the armhole, matching the front notches, back notches and underarm seams, as well as the sleeve cap notch to shoulder seam. Pin. Stitch around the armhole. Repeat for the other Sleeve. Press the seam allowances toward the Sleeve. Finish the seam allowances as desired.

FINISHING

50. Line up the side seams of the primary fabric and lining together at the Waist Tie. The seam allowances of the Waist Tie should already be pressed toward the back. Stitch in the ditch (page 20) at the Waist Tie through all the layers. Repeat for the other side seam at the other Waist Tie.

51. For the primary fabric, at the hem of the top or dress, fold and press ½ inch (1.25 cm) toward the wrong side twice. Edgestitch close to the first fold. Repeat for the lining.

52. Give the top or dress a good press and you are done!

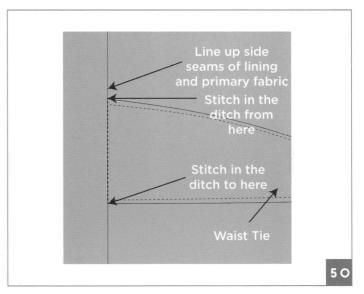

Line up side seams of lining and primary fabric

Stitch in the ditch from here

Stitch in the ditch to here

Waist Tie

50

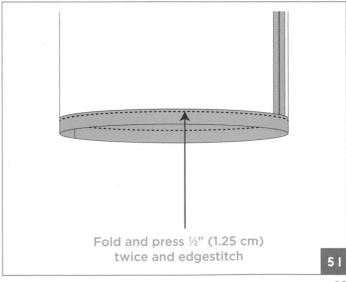

Fold and press ½" (1.25 cm) twice and edgestitch

51

THE TAKTSANG

You can call the Taktsang a jacket, a cardigan or a wrap; it's really all of the above! The Taktsang is designed for woven fabric and stable knit fabric. I like wearing my Taktsang in a quilted knit fabric as a warm jacket, but you can make it into a morning coverup by using lightweight silk. The Taktsang is an empty canvas where you can showcase your beautiful fabric!

The Taktsang has integrated, three-quarter-length dolman sleeves. The neckline is finished with facings. The hip-length bodice has a relaxed fit. A sash is included so you can tie it closed, but of course, you can choose to use your favorite belt instead of the self-fabric sash.

FRONT

BACK

CHOOSING YOUR SIZE

1. Compare your bust circumference (the fullest part of your measured bust) to the "Body Measurements" table. Choose the size that best fits your bust. If your measurement is between sizes, choose the smaller size if you like your garment more fitted; otherwise, choose the bigger size.

2. Compare your hip circumference (the fullest part of your measured hip) to the "Body Measurements" table. Choose the size that best fits your hips. If your measurement is between sizes, choose the smaller size if you like your garment more fitted; otherwise, choose the bigger size.

3. If you have different sizes for the bust and hip, you can blend sizes (page 11). The waist is designed to be very relaxed, and you do not have to consider the waist when selecting a size.

MATERIALS

PRIMARY FABRIC
Use a lightweight to medium-weight woven fabric with or without stretch. A stable knit fabric is also appropriate. Keep in mind that a fabric with stretch will result in a slightly larger garment.

INTERFACING
Use lightweight to medium-weight fusible woven or weft insertion interfacing (page 16).

BODY MEASUREMENTS

SIZE		OO	O	2	4	6	8	10	12	14	16	18	20
BUST	(IN)	31⅛	32½	33⅞	35⅛	36½	37⅞	39¼	40⅝	42	43¼	44⅝	46
	(CM)	79	82.5	86	89	92.5	96	99.5	103	106.5	110	113.5	117
HIP	(IN)	33¼	34⅝	35⅞	37¼	38⅝	40	41¼	42⅝	44	45⅜	46⅝	48
	(CM)	84.5	88	91	94.5	98	101.5	105	108	112	115	118.5	122

FINISHED GARMENT MEASUREMENTS

SIZE		OO	O	2	4	6	8	10	12	14	16	18	20
BUST*	(IN)	36¼	37¾	39⅜	40⅞	42½	44	45½	47⅛	48⅝	50¼	51¾	53¼
	(CM)	92	96	100	104	108	112	115.5	119.5	123.5	127.5	131.5	135.5
WAIST	(IN)	33⅝	35⅛	36⅝	38⅛	39⅝	41⅛	42⅝	44⅛	45⅝	47⅛	48⅝	50⅛
	(CM)	85.5	89	93	97	100.5	104.5	108	112	116	119.5	123.5	127
HIP	(IN)	36¼	37¾	39⅜	40⅞	42½	44	45½	47⅛	48⅝	50¼	51¾	53¼
	(CM)	92	96	100	104	108	112	115.5	119.5	123.5	127.5	131.5	135.5

*Because the garment is not restricted at the underarm, the bust measurements are estimated and serve only as a rough guideline.

FABRIC REQUIREMENTS

	OO	O	2	4	6	8	10	12	14	16	18	20
PRIMARY FABRIC (54 INCHES/137 CM WIDE)												
(YARD)	2½	2½	2½	2¾	2¾	2¾	2⅞	2⅞	2⅞	3	3	3
(CM)	230	230	230	250	250	250	265	265	265	275	275	275
INTERFACING (20 INCHES/51 CM WIDE)												
(YARD)	1⅛	1⅛	1⅛	1⅛	1⅛	1⅛	1¼	1¼	1¼	1¼	1¼	1¼
(CM)	105	105	105	105	105	105	115	115	115	120	120	120

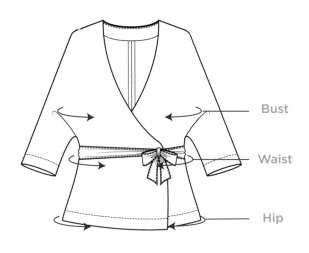

Bust

Waist

Hip

FABRIC CUTTING INSTRUCTIONS

PATTERN PIECE	FROM PRIMARY FABRIC, CUT	FROM INTERFACING, CUT
1 - Front	2 mirror images	0
2 - Back	2 mirror images	0
3 - Front Facing	2 mirror images	2 mirror images
4 - Back Facing	1	1
5 - Sash	2	0
6 - Belt Loop	3	0

LAYOUT DIAGRAMS

PRIMARY FABRIC

SIZES 00 TO 12

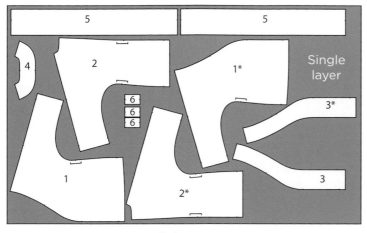

Selvage

Selvage

*Flip the pattern piece over to cut this piece

INTERFACING

ALL SIZES

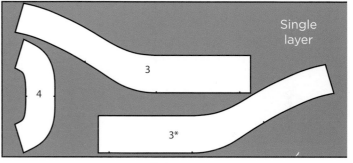

Selvage

Selvage

*Flip the pattern piece over to cut this piece

SIZES 14 TO 20

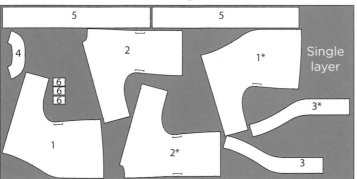

Selvage

Selvage

*Flip the pattern piece over to cut this piece

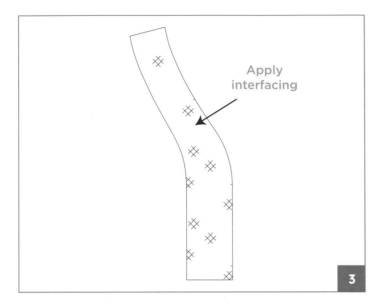

Apply
interfacing

3

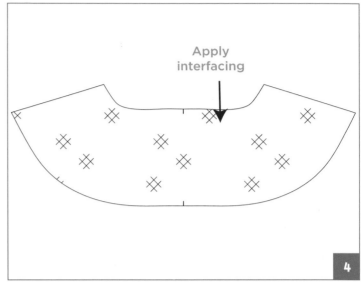

Apply
interfacing

4

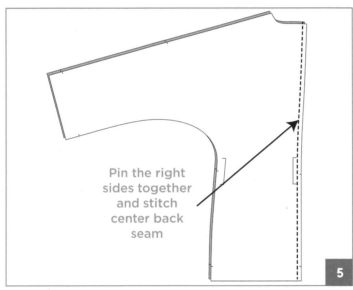

Pin the right
sides together
and stitch
center back
seam

5

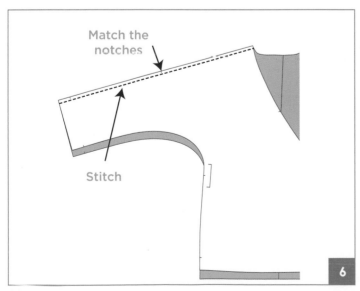

Match the
notches

Stitch

6

SEAM ALLOWANCES

The included seam allowances are ½ inch (1.25 cm) unless stated otherwise in the process.

PROCESS

CUTTING AND MARKING FABRIC

1. Trace the pattern outlines for your size onto a piece of paper (see back envelope), then cut the fabric according to the Layout Diagrams (page 43).

2. Transfer all the markings to the fabric before removing the pattern pieces from the fabric (pages 15–16).

STABILIZATION

3. Apply the interfacing on the wrong side of the Front Facing (3). Repeat for the other Front Facing.

4. Apply the interfacing on the wrong side of the Back Facing (4).

BACK

5. With the right sides together, pin the two pieces of the Back (2) together, matching the notches. Stitch. Using a hot iron, press the seam allowances open. Finish the seam allowances as desired (page 18). This seam is the center back.

SHOULDER

6. With the right sides together, pin the Front to the Back at the shoulder, matching the notches. Stitch. Press the seam allowances open. Finish the seam allowances. Repeat for the shoulder seam for the other Front and the other side of the Back.

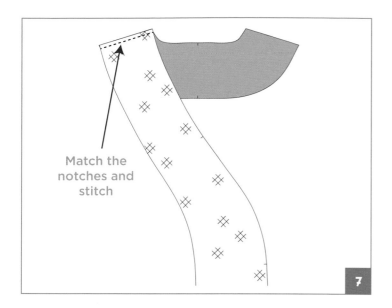

Match the
notches and
stitch

7

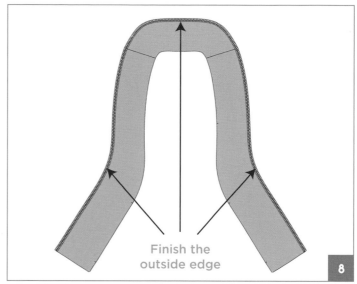

Finish the
outside edge

8

FACING

7. With the right sides together, pin the Front Facing to the Back Facing at the shoulder seam, matching the notches. Stitch. Press the seam allowances open. Finish the seam allowances as desired. Repeat for the other Front Facing and the other side of the Back Facing. We will refer to this assembled piece as the Facing below.

8. Finish the outside edge of the Facing as desired. The outside edge is the edge where the Front Facing has no notch.

9. With the right sides together, pin the Facing to the neckline of the assembled Front and Back, matching the notches and shoulder seams. The notch on the Back Facing should match the center back.

10. Stitch as pinned.

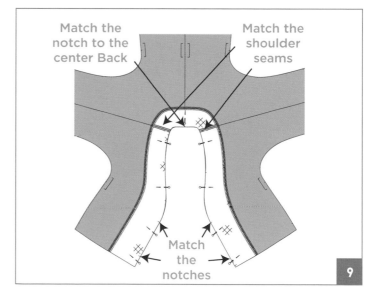

Match the
notch to the
center Back

Match the
shoulder
seams

Match
the
notches

9

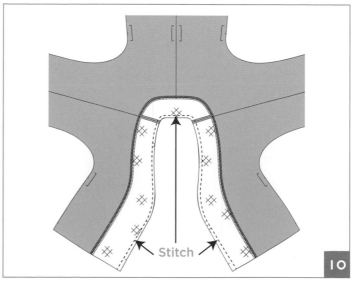

Stitch

10

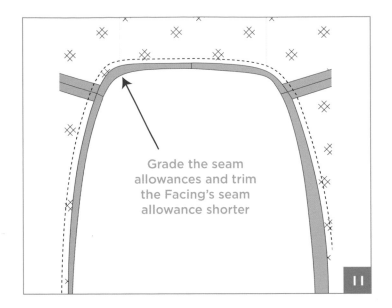

Grade the seam
allowances and trim
the Facing's seam
allowance shorter

11

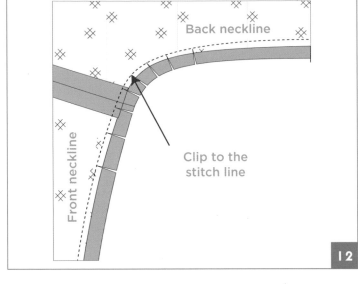

Back neckline

Front neckline

Clip to the
stitch line

12

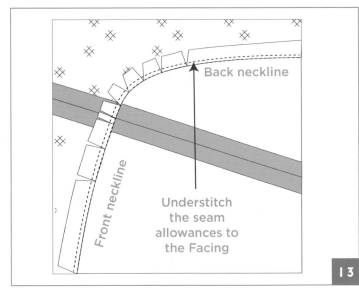

Back neckline

Front neckline

Understitch
the seam
allowances to
the Facing

13

11. Grade the seam allowances (page 18) with the
seam allowances of the Facing trimmed shorter.

12. At the curvier part of the neckline where the front
and back connect, using your scissors, clip to the
stitch line (page 18) every ¼ inch (6 mm) or so.
Take care not to clip beyond the stitch line.

13. Flip to the wrong side of the fabric. Open up the
Facing and press the seam allowances toward
the Facing. Understitch (page 19) the entire
neckline by stitching the seam allowances to
the Facing.

14. Fold the Facing toward the wrong side. Because of
the understitching, the seam naturally rolls slightly
toward the wrong side. Press.

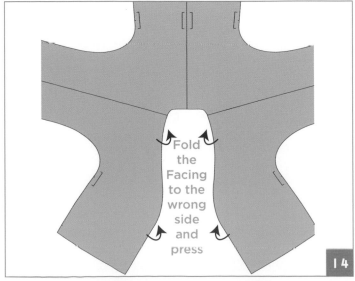

Fold
the
Facing
to the
wrong
side
and
press

14

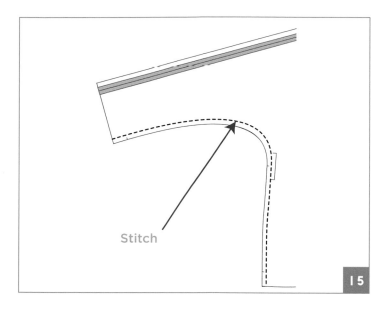

Stitch

15

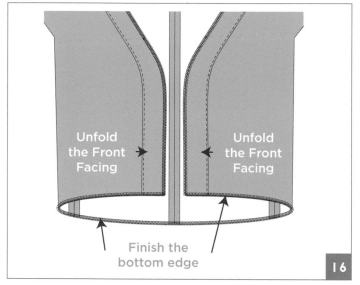

Unfold
the Front
Facing

Unfold
the Front
Facing

Finish the
bottom edge

16

SIDE

15. With the right sides together, pin the Front to the Back at the side and sleeve. Stitch. Press the seam allowances open. Finish the seam allowances as desired. Repeat for the other side and sleeve seam.

HEMMING

16. Unfold the Front Facing from the wrong side of the Front. Finish the bottom raw edge of the Front Facing, Front and Back as desired.

17. Turn the Front Facing to the right side of the Front. The seam allowances should be turned to the right side of the Front as well.

18. With a 1½-inch (3.8-cm) seam allowance, stitch the Front Facing to the Front at the bottom.

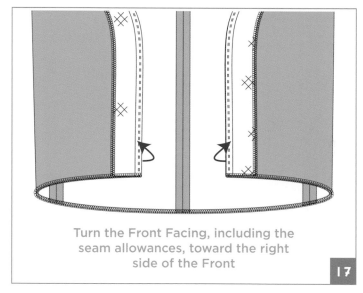

Turn the Front Facing, including the
seam allowances, toward the right
side of the Front

17

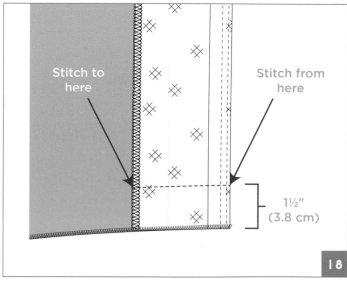

Stitch to
here

Stitch from
here

1½"
(3.8 cm)

18

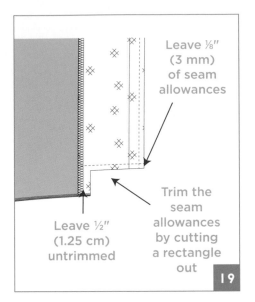

Leave ⅛"
(3 mm)
of seam
allowances

Trim the
seam
allowances
by cutting
a rectangle
out

Leave ½"
(1.25 cm)
untrimmed

19

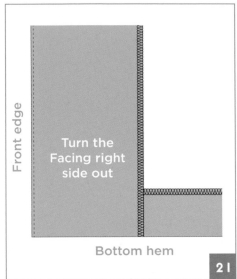

Front edge

Turn the
Facing right
side out

Bottom hem

21

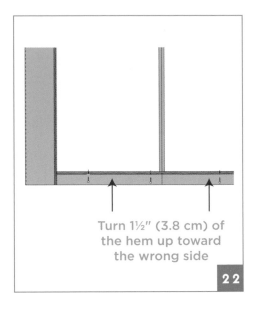

Turn 1½" (3.8 cm) of
the hem up toward
the wrong side

22

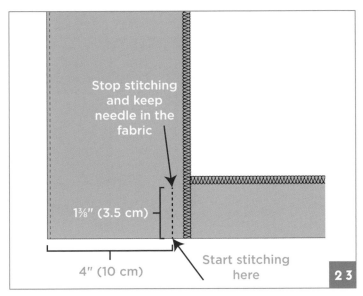

Stop stitching
and keep
needle in the
fabric

1⅜" (3.5 cm)

4" (10 cm)

Start stitching
here

23

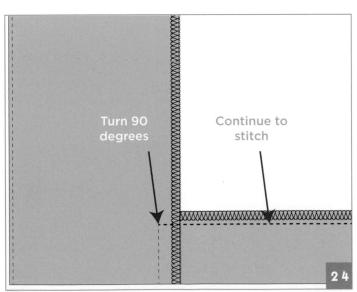

Turn 90
degrees

Continue to
stitch

24

19. Trim the seam allowances by cutting a rectangle out at the bottom corner so that only ⅛ inch (3 mm) of the seam allowances remain. Leave about ½ inch (1.25 cm) of the Front Facing untrimmed.

20. Repeat steps 18 and 19 for the other side of the Front and Front Facing.

21. Turn both Front Facings right side out. Part of the bottom hem will also be turned as a result.

22. Press the rest of the bottom hem up 1½ inches (3.8 cm) toward the wrong side. Pin.

23. At the point that is 4 inches (10 cm) from the front edge and at the very bottom, start stitching up for 1⅜ inches (3.5 cm) and stop with the needle down in the fabric, but do not cut the thread.

24. Turn 90 degrees toward the side seam and continue to stitch along the finished edge of the hem all the way around the entire garment's edge.

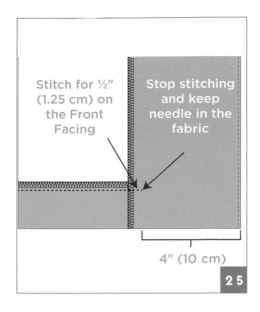

Stitch for ½" (1.25 cm) on the Front Facing

Stop stitching and keep needle in the fabric

4" (10 cm)

25

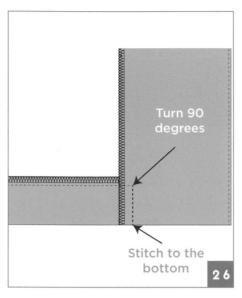

Turn 90 degrees

Stitch to the bottom

26

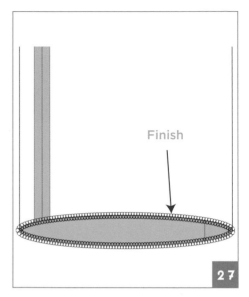

Finish

27

25. When you reach the other Front Facing on the opposite side, stitch on the Front Facing for ½ inch (1.25 cm), which should match the 4-inch (10-cm) mark on the opposite Front. Stop with the needle down in the fabric, but do not cut the thread.

26. Turn 90 degrees again toward the bottom. Stitch toward the bottom.

SLEEVE HEM

27. Finish the bottom edge of the sleeve as desired.

28. Fold and press the hem 1½ inches (3.8 cm) up toward the wrong side.

29. Topstitch (page 20) 1⅜ inches (3.5 cm) from the fold of the hem. It will be easier if you turn the garment wrong side out and stitch with the presser foot against the inside (the right side) of the sleeve.

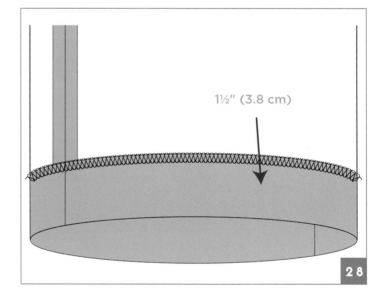

1½" (3.8 cm)

28

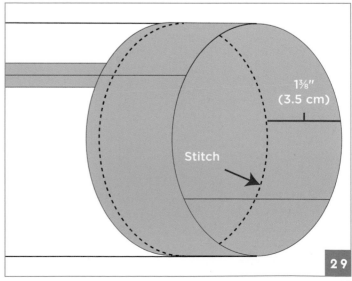

1⅜" (3.5 cm)

Stitch

29

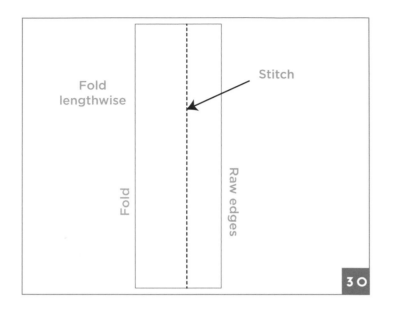

Stitch

Fold
lengthwise

Fold

Raw edges

30

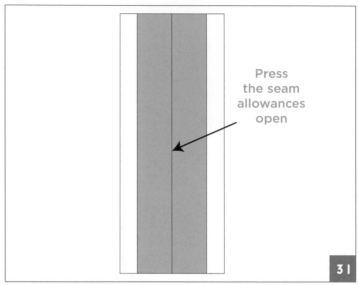

Press
the seam
allowances
open

31

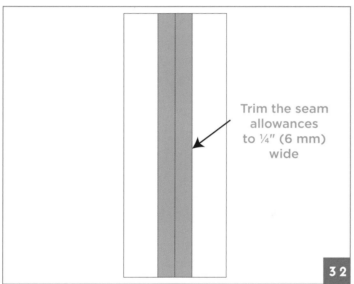

Trim the seam
allowances
to ¼" (6 mm)
wide

32

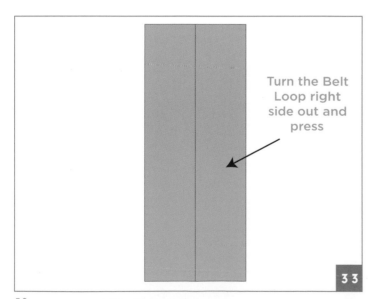

Turn the Belt
Loop right
side out and
press

33

BELT LOOP

30. With the right sides inside, fold the Belt Loop (6) in half lengthwise. Stitch.

31. Press the Belt Loop so that the seam is in the middle of the Belt Loop with the seam allowances open.

32. Trim both seam allowances to ¼ inch (6 mm) wide.

33. Turn the Belt Loop right side out and press.

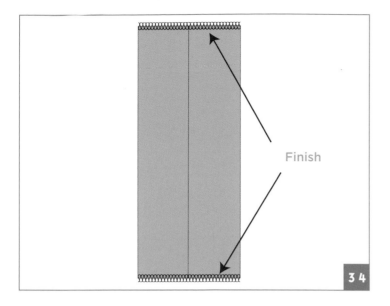

Finish

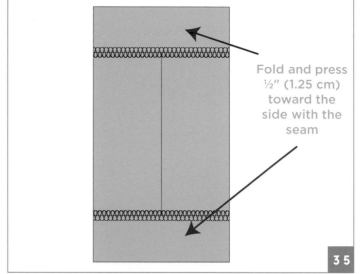

Fold and press ½" (1.25 cm) toward the side with the seam

34. Finish the top and bottom raw edges as desired.

35. Fold and press ½ inch (1.25 cm) of each end toward the side with the seam.

36. Repeat steps 30 to 35 for the other two Belt Loop pieces.

37. Pin the Belt Loop pieces over the belt loop placement markings at the waist—one over the left-side seam, one over the right-side seam and one over the center back seam. You can also try on the garment and pin the Belt Loop pieces higher or lower as necessary.

38. Edgestitch (page 20) close to the folds made in step 35. Be sure to stitch back and forth at the beginning and the end of the stitch lines to secure them.

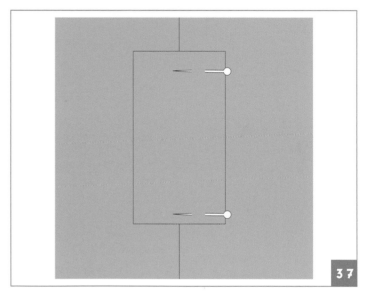

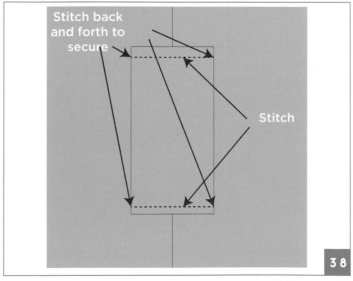

Stitch back and forth to secure

Stitch

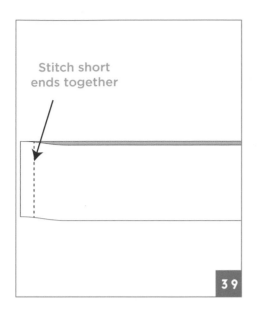

Stitch short
ends together

39

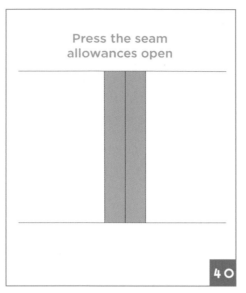

Press the seam
allowances open

40

Press ½″ (1.25 cm)
toward the wrong side

41

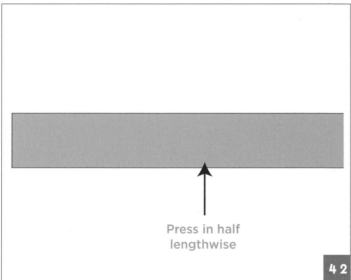

Press in half
lengthwise

42

SASH

39. With the right sides together, pin the short ends of the two Sash (5) pieces together. Stitch.

40. Press the seam allowances open.

41. Fold and press ½ inch (1.25 cm) of the short end toward the wrong side. Repeat for the other short end.

42. With the wrong side inside, fold and press the Sash in half lengthwise to create a middle crease.

43. Open the Sash at the middle crease. With the wrong side inside, bring one long raw edge to the middle crease and press.

Bring the raw edge to the middle
crease and press

43

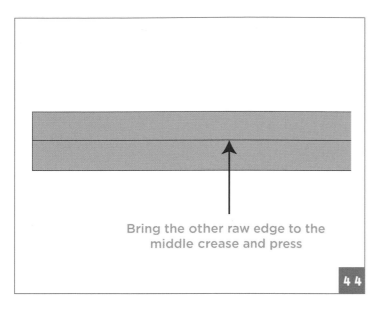

Bring the other raw edge to the
middle crease and press

44

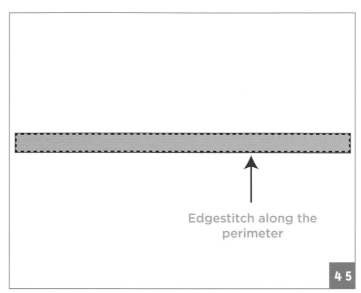

Edgestitch along the
perimeter

45

44. Bring the other long raw edge to the middle
crease and press.

45. Close the middle fold made in step 42 again, so all
the raw edges are enclosed. Edgestitch along the
perimeter of the Sash. Press.

FINISHING

46. Hand sew a few stitches to tack the facing to the
shoulder seam allowances and center back seam
allowances.

47. Alternatively, you can stitch along the entire
outline of the facing through the Front and Back
to secure it.

48. Give the garment a good press and you are done!

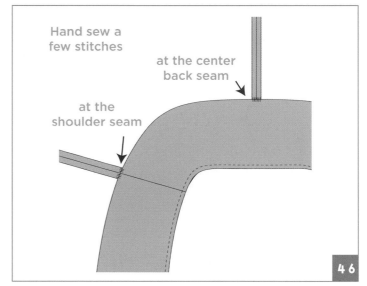

Hand sew a
few stitches

at the center
back seam

at the
shoulder seam

46

47

THE PRAGUE

I didn't expect to like the cold shoulder style as much as I do. I think it adds a wow factor to an otherwise plain garment. I made a woven pattern with cold shoulders a few years back, but the Prague Top & Dress pattern is designed for knit fabric, which is a little more casual. Besides, the Prague is a pullover style, which means no zipper and no buttons!

The Prague comes in different variations—the cold shoulder top includes scoop neck, top length and short sleeves, and the cold shoulder dress includes V neck, dress length and three-quarter-length sleeves. I group various features into two variations for simplicity's sake, but in fact, the necklines, sleeve lengths and bodice lengths could be mixed and matched, so it's possible to have eight different looks!

Both the cold shoulder hole and the neckline are finished with bands. The top is hip length, whereas the dress hits slightly above the knees. The garment is semi-fitted at the bust and above but is more relaxed in the midsection and below.

COLD SHOULDER TOP
(SEE PHOTO ON PAGE 22)

FRONT   BACK

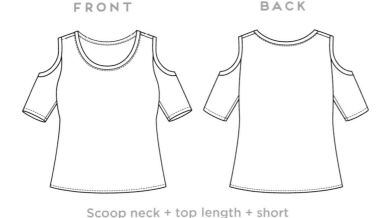

Scoop neck + top length + short sleeves

COLD SHOULDER DRESS
(SEE PHOTO ON PAGE 54)

FRONT   BACK

V neck + dress length + three-quarter-length sleeves

CHOOSING YOUR SIZE

1. Compare your bust circumference (the fullest part of your measured bust) to the "Body Measurements" table. Choose the size that best fits your bust. If your measurement is between sizes, choose the smaller size if you like your garment more fitted; otherwise, choose the bigger size.

2. Compare your waist circumference (the narrowest part of your measured waist) to the "Body Measurements" table. Choose the size that best fits your waist. If your measurement is between sizes, choose the smaller size if you like your garment more fitted; otherwise, choose the bigger size.

3. Compare your hip circumference (the fullest part of your measured hip) to the "Body Measurements" table. Choose the size that best fits your hips. If your measurement is between sizes, choose the smaller size if you like your garment more fitted; otherwise, choose the bigger size.

4. If you have different sizes for the bust, waist and hip, you can blend sizes (page 11).

MATERIALS

PRIMARY FABRIC
Use a very lightweight to medium-weight knit fabric with 40 to 60 percent horizontal stretch (page 10) and good recovery. Jersey, rayon spandex, double brushed polyester and cotton spandex are good choices.

OTHER MATERIALS
9 inches (23 cm) of ⅜-inch (1-cm)- or ½-inch (1.25-cm)-wide straight fusible stay tape (page 16); you can also cut your own using lightweight woven fusible interfacing on the straight grain.

BODY MEASUREMENTS

SIZE		00	0	2	4	6	8	10	12	14	16	18	20
BUST	(IN)	31⅛	32½	33⅞	35⅛	36½	37⅞	39¼	40⅝	42	43¼	44⅝	46
	(CM)	79	82.5	86	89	92.5	96	99.5	103	106.5	110	113.5	117
WAIST	(IN)	25⅜	26¾	28⅛	29½	30⅞	32¼	33⅝	35	36⅜	37¾	39⅛	40½
	(CM)	64.5	68	71.5	75	78.5	82	85.5	89	92.5	96	99.5	103
HIP	(IN)	33¼	34⅝	35⅞	37¼	38⅝	40	41¼	42⅝	44	45⅜	46⅝	48
	(CM)	84.5	88	91	94.5	98	101.5	105	108	112	115.5	118.5	122

FINISHED GARMENT MEASUREMENTS

SIZE		00	0	2	4	6	8	10	12	14	16	18	20
BUST	(IN)	31	32½	34	35½	37	38½	40	41½	43	44½	46	47½
	(CM)	79	82.5	86.5	90	94	98	101.5	105.5	109.5	113	117	121
WAIST	(IN)	29½	31	32½	33⅞	35⅜	36⅞	38⅜	39⅞	41¼	42¾	44¼	45¾
	(CM)	75	78.5	82.5	86	90	93.5	97.5	101.5	105	108.5	112.5	116
HIP	(IN)	37⅜	38⅞	40⅜	41⅞	43⅜	44⅞	46⅜	47⅞	49⅜	50⅞	52⅜	53⅞
	(CM)	95	99	102.5	106.5	110.5	114	118	121.5	125.5	129.5	133	137

FABRIC REQUIREMENTS

		00	0	2	4	6	8	10	12	14	16	18	20
PRIMARY FABRIC (54 INCHES/137 CM WIDE)													
COLD SHOULDER TOP	(YARD)	1	1	1	1½	1½	1½	1¾	1¾	1¾	1⅞	1⅞	1⅞
	(CM)	90	90	90	135	135	135	160	160	160	170	170	170
COLD SHOULDER DRESS	(YARD)	1¾	1¾	1¾	1⅞	1⅞	1⅞	2⅛	2⅛	2⅛	2⅝	2⅝	2⅝
	(CM)	160	160	160	170	170	170	195	195	195	240	240	240

FABRIC CUTTING INSTRUCTIONS

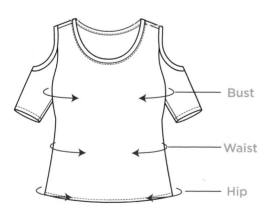

PATTERN PIECE	FROM PRIMARY FABRIC, CUT
1 - Front	1 on fold*
2 - Back	1 on fold*
3 - Sleeve	2 mirror images*
4 - Neckband (for Cold Shoulder Top only)	1 on fold
5 - Neckband (for Cold Shoulder Dress only)	1 on fold
6 - Shoulder Hole Band	2 on fold

*Use the hem, sleeve hem and neckline marked "Cut Here for Cold Shoulder Top" or "Cut Here for Cold Shoulder Dress" for your chosen variation.

LAYOUT DIAGRAMS

COLD SHOULDER TOP

SIZES OO TO 8

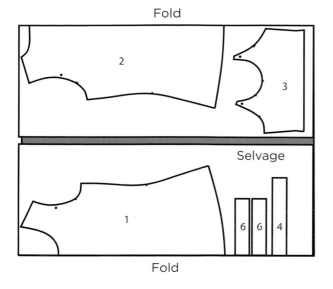

SIZES IO TO 20

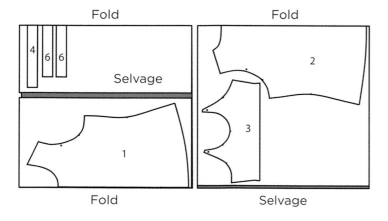

COLD SHOULDER DRESS

SIZES OO TO 8

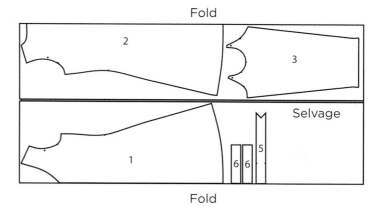

SIZES IO TO 20

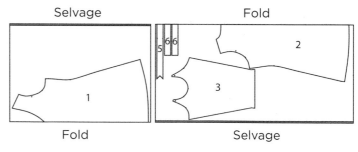

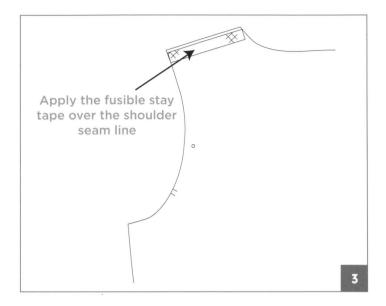

Apply the fusible stay tape over the shoulder seam line

3

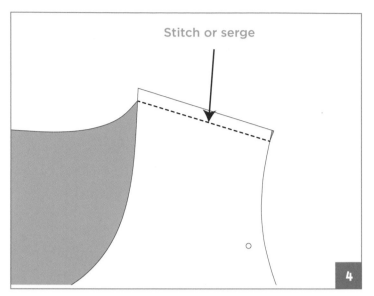

Stitch or serge

4

SEAM ALLOWANCES

The included seam allowances are ⅜ inch (1 cm) unless stated otherwise in the process.

PROCESS

CUTTING AND MARKING FABRIC

1. Trace the pattern outlines for your size and option onto a piece of paper (see back envelope), then cut the fabric according to the Layout Diagrams (page 57).

2. Transfer all the markings to the fabric before removing the pattern pieces from the fabric (pages 15–16).

STABILIZATION

3. Cut a length of fusible stay tape and, using a hot iron, apply it onto the Back (2) shoulder on the wrong side, centered over the seam line. The seam line is ⅜ inch (1 cm) from the cut edge. Repeat for the other Back shoulder.

SHOULDER

4. With the right sides together, pin the Front (1) to the Back at the shoulder. Stitch or serge. If you stitched the seam, press the seam allowances open using a hot iron and finish the seam allowances (page 18). If you serged the seam, press the seam allowances toward the Back. Repeat for the other shoulder.

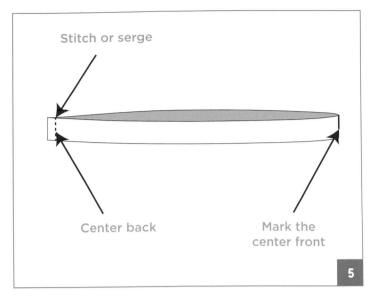

Stitch or serge

Center back

Mark the center front

5

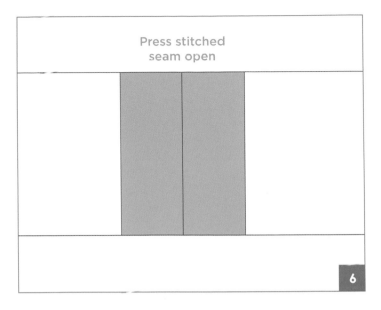

Press stitched seam open

6

NECKLINE

For the Cold Shoulder Top's scoop neckline, follow steps 5 to 14. For the Cold Shoulder Dress's V neckline, skip to step 15.

5. With the right side inside, pin the short ends of the Neckband (4) together. Stitch or serge to form a loop. This seam is the center back seam. The opposite end, where the fabric was folded, is the center front. Mark the center front if it's not already marked.

6. If you stitched the seam, press the seam allowances open.

7. If you serged the seam, use your scissors to clip the seam allowances in the middle (but not through the seam), and press one portion to one side and the remaining portion to the other side. This reduces the bulk of the seam.

8. Fold the Neckband lengthwise with the wrong side inside to create a narrower loop. Press.

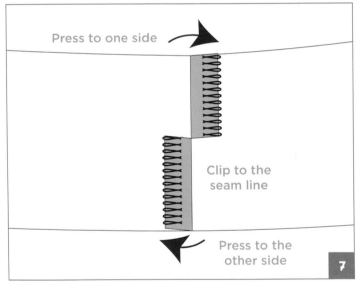

Press to one side

Clip to the seam line

Press to the other side

7

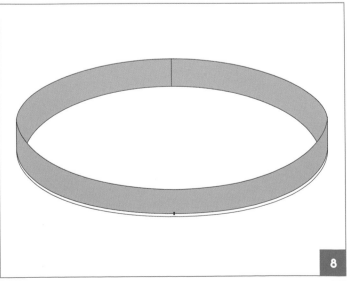

8

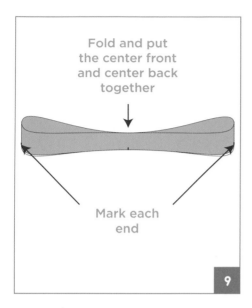

Fold and put the center front and center back together

Mark each end

9

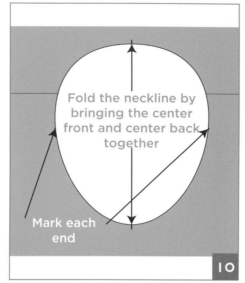

Fold the neckline by bringing the center front and center back together

Mark each end

10

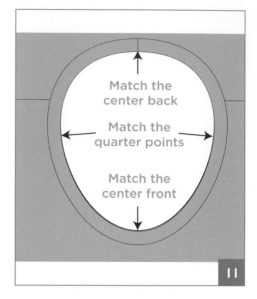

Match the center back

Match the quarter points

Match the center front

11

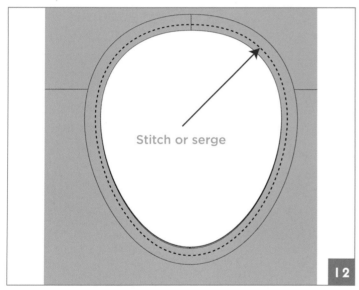

Stitch or serge

12

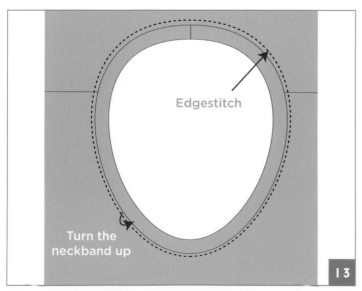

Edgestitch

Turn the neckband up

13

9. Identify the quarter points of the Neckband by bringing the center front and center back together. Mark the fold at each end.

10. Similarly, identify the quarter points of the neckline by bringing the center front and center back points together. Mark the fold at each end. Note that the shoulder seams are not the quarter points.

11. Pin the Neckband onto the right side of the Front and Back neckline, matching the raw edges of the Neckband to the neckline, as well as stretching to match the quarter points, which include the center back to center back, center front to center front and the additional points you marked in steps 9 and 10.

12. Stitch or serge. If you stitched the seam, finish the seam allowance.

13. Turn the Neckband up and press the seam allowances toward the Front and Back. From the right side, edgestitch (page 20) along the neckline so that you stitch onto the Front or Back through the seam allowances underneath. Press.

14. Skip to step 28 to continue.

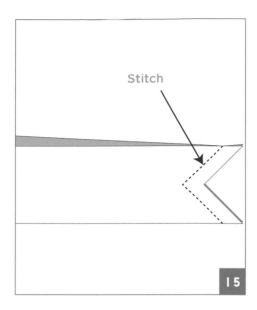

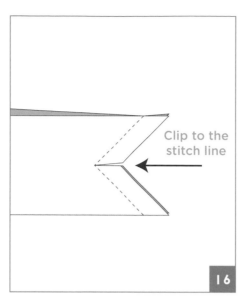

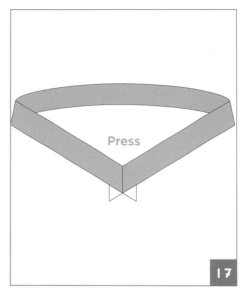

Follow steps 15 to 27 for the Cold Shoulder Dress's V neckline.

15. With the right sides inside, pin and stitch the V-shaped seam of Neckband (5) together, forming a loop.

16. Using your scissors, clip the V of Neckband to, but not beyond, the stitch line.

17. Fold the Neckband in half lengthwise with the wrong sides together. Press. The seam allowances should be pressed open.

18. On the Front, mark the ⅜-inch (1-cm) seam line accurately at the point of the V neck through the center of the circle. The mark on each side of the V should be about 1 inch (2.5 cm) or so long.

19. Stay stitch (page 20) exactly on the V as you marked in step 18, pivoting at the point of the V.

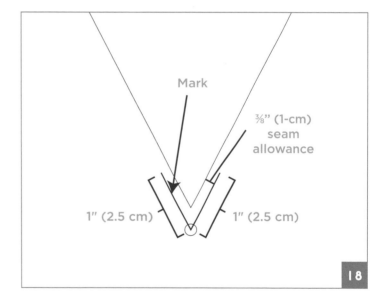

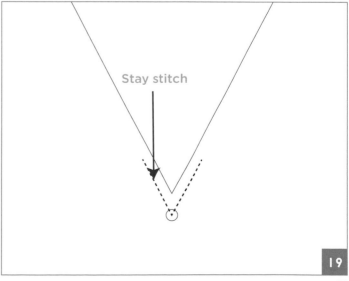

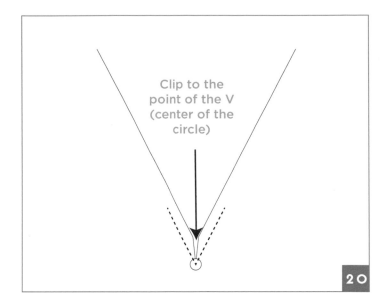

Clip to the point of the V (center of the circle)

20

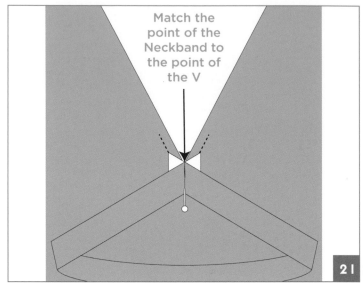

Match the point of the Neckband to the point of the V

21

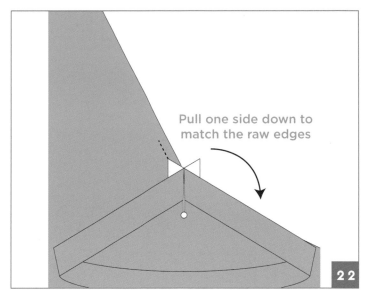

Pull one side down to match the raw edges

22

20. Using your scissors, clip to, but not beyond, the stitch line at the point of the V.

21. With the Front right side up, pin the center seam of the Neckband to the neckline, with the point of the Neckband aligning with the point of the V on the neckline (not the bottom of the clip that you made). Be sure that the Neckband seam is vertical.

22. Pull one side of the Front V neck downward so you are spreading open the clip of the Front until one side of the neckline aligns with one side of the Neckband, with the raw edges even.

23. Turn over to the wrong side so you can see the stay stitching; stitch exactly over the stay stitch on one side of the V through all layers.

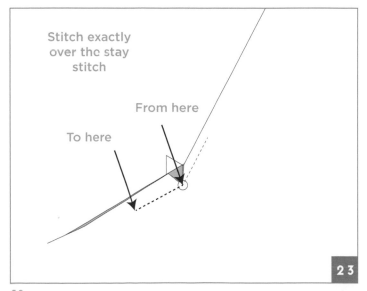

Stitch exactly over the stay stitch

From here

To here

23

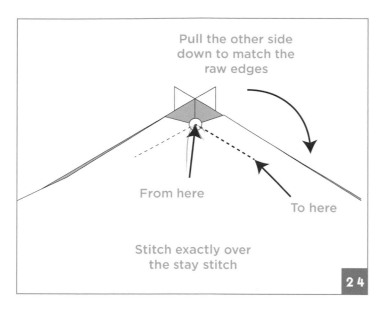

Pull the other side down to match the raw edges

From here

To here

Stitch exactly over the stay stitch

24

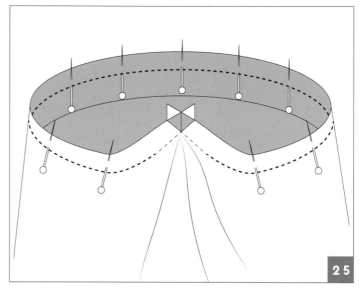

25

24. Align the other side of the neckline with the Neckband, with the raw edges even. From the wrong side of the Front, where the line of stay stitch is visible, stitch exactly over the stay stitch on the remaining side of the V through all layers.

25. Stretch to pin the rest of the Neckband along the neckline of the Front and Back, with the notches on the Neckband aligned with shoulder seams and the center backs aligned. Note that you will need to stretch the Neckband more on the back portion than the front portion.

26. Stitch around the neckline through all layers, being sure to connect with the V previously stitched. Press the seam allowances toward the Front and Back. Finish the neckline seam.

27. From the right side, edgestitch (page 20) next to the Neckband on the Front and Back through the seam allowances underneath, starting from the point of the V, around the back neckline and ending at the point of the V. Press.

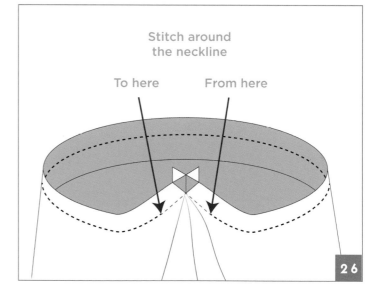

Stitch around the neckline

To here   From here

26

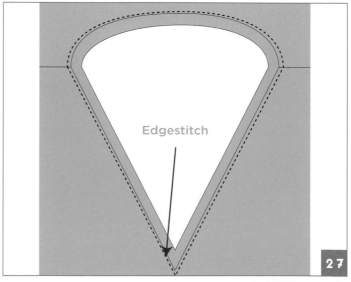

Edgestitch

27

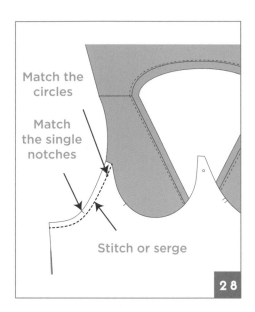

Match the
circles

Match
the single
notches

Stitch or serge

28

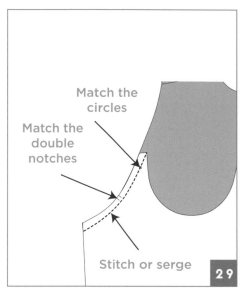

Match the
circles

Match the
double
notches

Stitch or serge

29

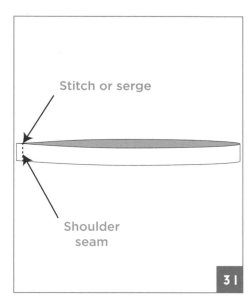

Stitch or serge

Shoulder
seam

31

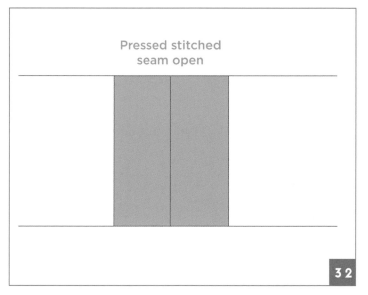

Pressed stitched
seam open

32

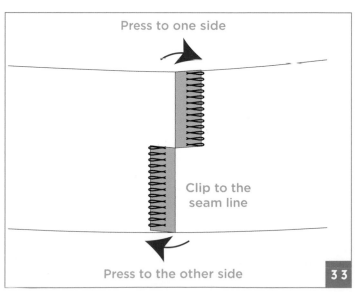

Press to one side

Clip to the
seam line

Press to the other side

33

SLEEVES

28. With the right sides together, pin the Sleeve (3) to
the Front, matching the circles and single notches.
Stitch or serge. Press the seam allowances toward
the Sleeve. Finish the seam allowances if you
stitched the seam.

29. With the right sides together, pin the Sleeve to the
Back, matching the circles and double notches.
Stitch or serge. Press the seam allowances toward
the Sleeve. Finish the seam allowances if you
stitched the seam.

30. Repeat steps 28 and 29 for the other Sleeve.

31. With the right side inside, pin the short ends of the
Shoulder Hole Band (6) together. Stitch or serge
to form a loop. This seam is the shoulder seam.

32. If you stitched the seam, press the seam
allowances open.

33. If you serged the seam, clip the seam allowances
in the middle (but not through the seam) and
press one portion to one side and the remaining
portion to the other side. This reduces the bulk of
the seam.

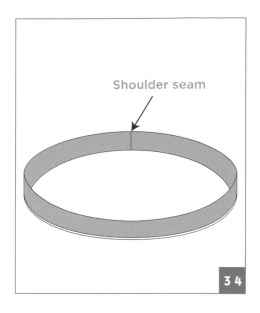

Shoulder seam

3 4

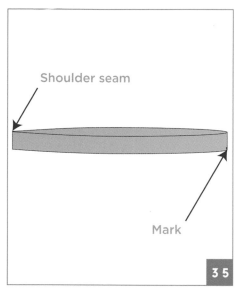

Shoulder seam

Mark

3 5

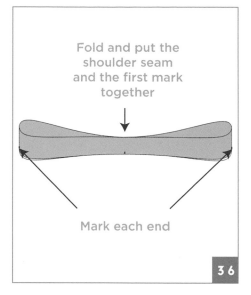

Fold and put the shoulder seam and the first mark together

Mark each end

3 6

3 4. Fold the Shoulder Hole Band lengthwise with the wrong side inside to create a narrower loop. Press.

3 5. Identify the quarter points of the Shoulder Hole Band by folding it with the seam at one end. Mark the opposite end.

3 6. Bring the mark together with the seam. Mark the fold at each end. Now you have three marks and one seam; those are the quarter points.

3 7. Similarly, identify the quarter points of the shoulder hole. First, fold the shoulder hole with the shoulder seam at one end. Mark the opposite end.

3 8. Then bring the mark together with the seam. Mark the fold at each end. Now you have three marks and one seam; those are the quarter points.

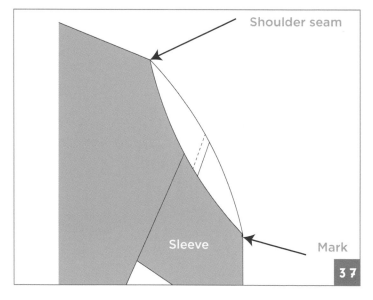

Shoulder seam

Sleeve

Mark

3 7

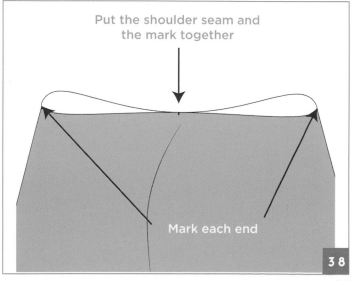

Put the shoulder seam and the mark together

Mark each end

3 8

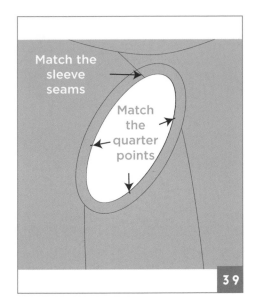

Match the sleeve seams

Match the quarter points

39

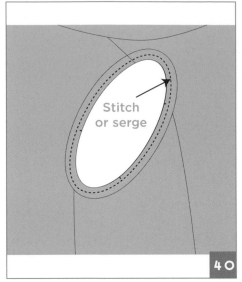

Stitch or serge

40

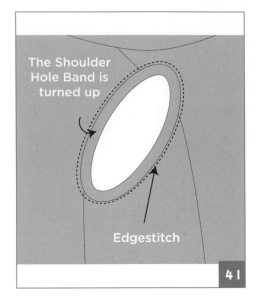

The Shoulder Hole Band is turned up

Edgestitch

41

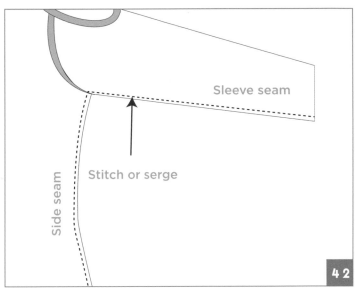

Sleeve seam

Side seam

Stitch or serge

42

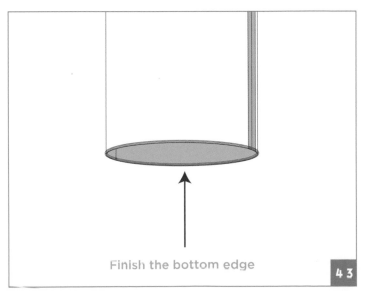

Finish the bottom edge

43

39. Pin the Shoulder Hole Band onto the right side of the shoulder hole, matching the raw edges of the Shoulder Hole Band to the shoulder hole, as well as stretching to match the quarter points, which include the shoulder seams and the three points you marked.

40. Stitch or serge. Turn the Shoulder Hole Band up and press the seam allowances toward the Front, Back and Sleeve. If you stitched the seam, finish the seam allowance.

41. From the right side, edgestitch along the shoulder hole, so that you stitch onto the Front, Back and Sleeve through the seam allowances underneath. Press.

42. With the right sides together, pin the Front to the Back, matching notches and underarm seams. Stitch or serge from the bottom edge of the Front and Back to the bottom edge of the Sleeve. If you stitched the seam, press the seam allowances open and finish the seam allowances. If you serged the seam, press it toward the Back.

43. Finish the bottom cut edge of the Sleeve.

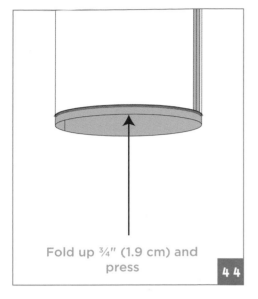

Fold up ¾″ (1.9 cm) and press

44

Edgestitch

45

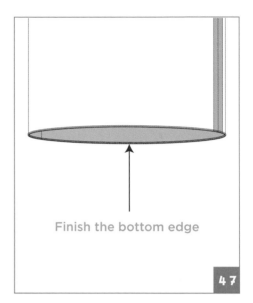

Finish the bottom edge

47

44. Fold and press ¾ inch (1.9 cm) toward the wrong side.

45. Edgestitch close to the cut edge.

46. Repeat steps 31 to 45 for the other Sleeve.

FINISHING

47. Finish the bottom cut edge of the garment.

48. Fold and press ¾ inch (1.9 cm) toward the wrong side.

49. Edgestitch close to the cut edge.

50. Give the top or dress a good press and you are done!

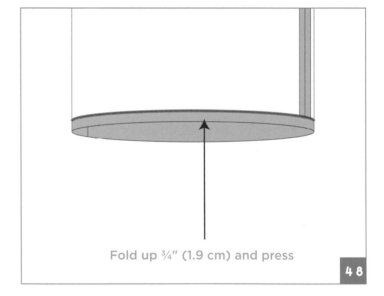

Fold up ¾″ (1.9 cm) and press

48

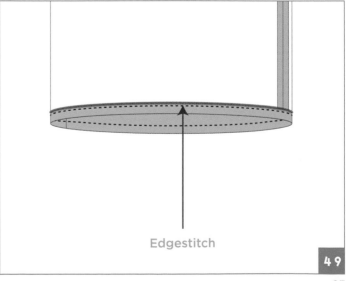

Edgestitch

49

THE CARLSBAD

Simple and elegant are the perfect adjectives for the Carlsbad Cardigan. Designed for knit fabric with good recovery, the Carlsbad has a soft draped front and hi-lo hemline. You can choose to lengthen or shorten the cardigan for different looks. It also comes in a vest option!

DRAPED CARDIGAN
(SEE PHOTO ON PAGE 68)

FRONT   BACK

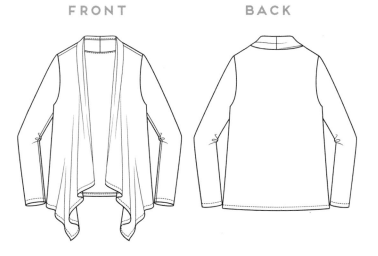

DRAPED VEST
(SEE PHOTO ON PAGE 4)

FRONT   BACK

CHOOSING YOUR SIZE

1. Compare your bust circumference (the fullest part of your measured bust) to the "Body Measurements" table. Choose the size that best fits your bust. If you are between sizes, choose the smaller size if you like your garment more fitted; otherwise, choose the bigger size.

2. There is no need to blend sizes; use the same size for the entire cardigan.

MATERIALS

PRIMARY FABRIC

Use a lightweight to medium-weight, two- or four-way stretch knit fabric with great recovery and 50 to 100 percent horizontal stretch (page 10). Keep in mind that the more stretch and drape a fabric has, the longer the cardigan will be (and vice versa). Both the right side and wrong side of the fabric will be visible when the cardigan is worn; choose your fabric accordingly.

OTHER MATERIALS

29 inches (74 cm) of ⅜-inch (1-cm)-wide straight fusible stay tape (page 16); you can also cut your own using lightweight woven fusible interfacing on the straight grain.

BODY MEASUREMENTS

SIZE		OO	O	2	4	6	8	10	12	14	16	18	20
BUST	(IN)	31⅛	32½	33⅞	35⅛	36½	37⅞	39¼	40⅝	42	43¼	44⅝	46
	(CM)	79	82.5	86	89	92.5	96	99.5	103	106.5	110	113.5	117

FINISHED GARMENT MEASUREMENTS

SIZE		OO	O	2	4	6	8	10	12	14	16	18	20
BUST	(IN)	31⅛	32⅝	34⅛	35½	37	38⅜	39⅞	41⅜	42¾	44¼	45¾	47⅛
	(CM)	79	83	86.5	90	94	97.5	101.5	105	108.5	112.5	116	120
BACK LENGTH	(IN)	23¼	23½	23⅞	24⅛	24½	24¾	25⅛	25⅜	25¾	26	26⅜	26⅝
	(CM)	59	60	60.5	61.5	62	63	64	64.5	65.5	66	67	67.5

FABRIC REQUIREMENTS

		OO	O	2	4	6	8	10	12	14	16	18	20
PRIMARY FABRIC (54 INCHES/137 CM WIDE)													
DRAPED CARDIGAN	(YARD)	1⅝	1⅝	1⅝	1⅝	1⅝	1⅝	1¾	1¾	1¾	2⅛	2⅛	2⅛
	(CM)	150	150	150	150	150	150	160	160	160	195	195	195
DRAPED VEST	(YARD)	1⅜	1⅜	1⅜	1½	1½	1½	1⅝	1⅝	1⅝	1¾	1¾	1¾
	(CM)	125	125	125	135	135	135	150	150	150	160	160	160

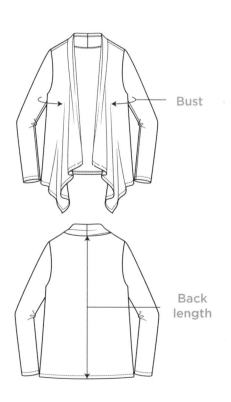

Bust

Back length

FABRIC CUTTING INSTRUCTIONS

PATTERN PIECE	FROM PRIMARY FABRIC, CUT
1 - Front*	2 mirror images
2 - Back	1 on fold
3 - Sleeve (for the Draped Cardigan option only)	2 mirror images
4 - Arm Band (for the Draped Vest option only)	2 mirror images

*Cut corresponding armhole for the Draped Cardigan or Draped Vest option.

LAYOUT DIAGRAMS

DRAPED CARDIGAN

SIZES OO TO 12

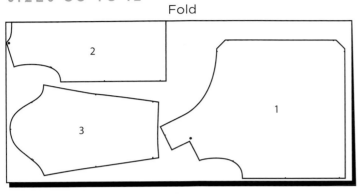

SIZES 14 TO 16

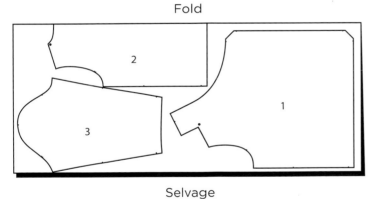

SIZES 18 TO 20

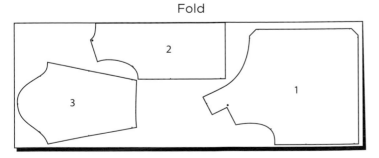

DRAPED VEST

SIZES OO TO 16

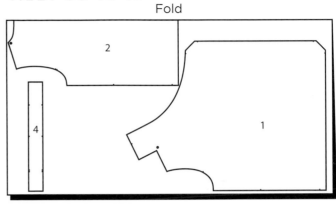

SIZES 18 TO 20

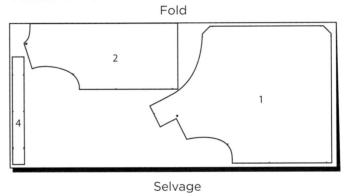

Apply the fusible stay, centered over the shoulder seams

3

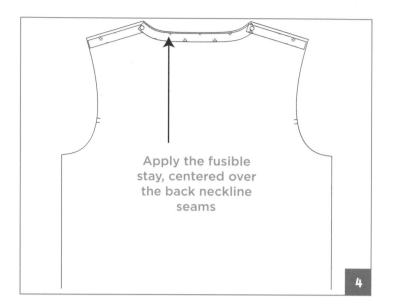

Apply the fusible stay, centered over the back neckline seams

4

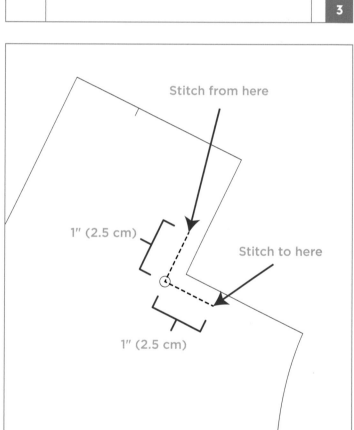

Stitch from here

1" (2.5 cm)

Stitch to here

1" (2.5 cm)

5

SEAM ALLOWANCES

The included seam allowances are ⅜ inch (1 cm) unless stated otherwise in the process.

PROCESS

CUTTING AND MARKING FABRIC

1. Trace the pattern outlines for your size and option onto a piece of paper (see back envelope), then cut the fabric according to the Layout Diagrams (page 71).

2. Transfer all the markings to the fabric before removing the pattern pieces (pages 15–16).

STABILIZATION

3. Cut a piece of fusible interfacing that is as long as the back shoulder. Using a hot iron, apply the fusible interfacing over the shoulder seam on the wrong side of the Back (2). Repeat for the other shoulder.

4. Similarly, cut a piece of fusible interfacing that is as long as the back neckline. Apply the fusible interfacing over the back neckline seam on the wrong side of the Back.

FRONT, SHOULDER AND BACK

5. Reinforce the right angle of the shoulder corner on the Front (1). To do so, start to stitch on the seam line 1 inch (2.5 cm) toward the circle. When getting to the center of the circle, put the needle down and lift up the presser foot to pivot 90 degrees. Then put the presser foot back down to continue to stitch 1 inch (2.5 cm) away from the circle. Repeat for the other Front.

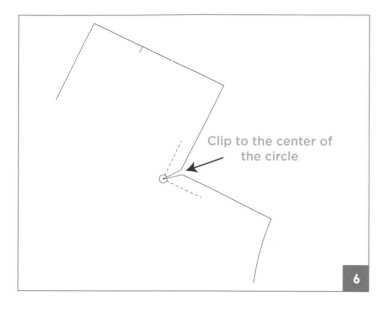

Clip to the center of the circle

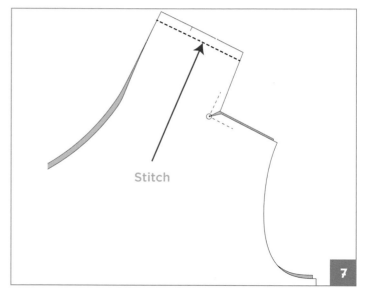

Stitch

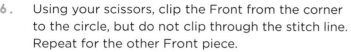

6. Using your scissors, clip the Front from the corner to the circle, but do not clip through the stitch line. Repeat for the other Front piece.

7. With the right sides together, pin the two pieces of the Front at the back neck, matching the notches. Stitch or serge. If you stitched the seam, using a hot iron, press the seam allowances open. If you serged the seam, press the serged seam allowances to one side.

8. With the right sides together, pin the Front to the Back at the shoulder, matching the outer shoulder and circles. Stitch from the outer shoulder to the circle. Press the seam allowances toward the Back. Repeat for the other shoulder.

9. With the right sides together, pin the Front and Back at the back neckline between the circles. You will need to stretch the fabric so that the clip you made in step 6 is spread open slightly to match the circles. Stitch from one circle to the other circle. Press the seam allowances toward the Back. Finish the shoulder seams and the back neck seam (page 18).

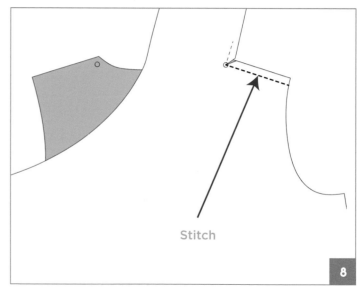

Stitch

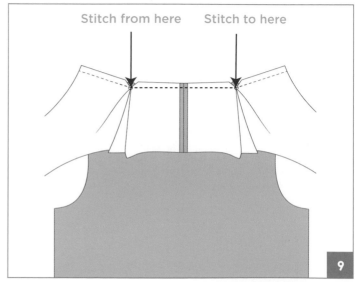

Stitch from here   Stitch to here

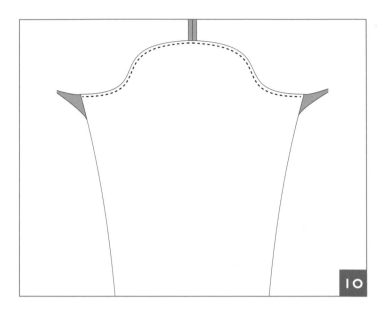

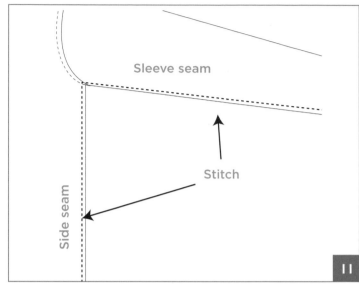

Side seam

Sleeve seam

Stitch

10

11

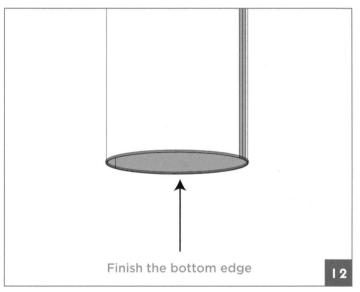

Finish the bottom edge

12

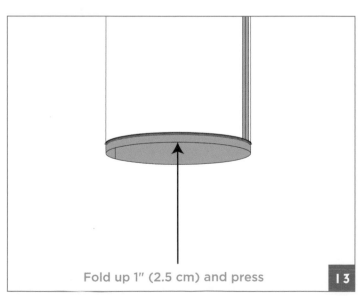

Fold up 1" (2.5 cm) and press

13

FOR THE DRAPED CARDIGAN OPTION

10. With the right sides together, pin the Sleeve (3) to the armhole, matching the center notch to the shoulder seam, as well as matching the single notches and the double notches. Stitch or serge. If you choose to stitch, finish the seam. Press the seam allowances toward the Sleeve.

11. With the right sides together, pin the Front to the Back, matching the notches and the underarm seams. Stitch or serge from the bottom edge of the side seam to the bottom edge of the Sleeve. If you choose to stitch, finish the seam allowances. Press the seam allowances toward the Back.

12. Finish the bottom cut edge of the Sleeve.

13. Fold and press 1 inch (2.5 cm) toward the wrong side.

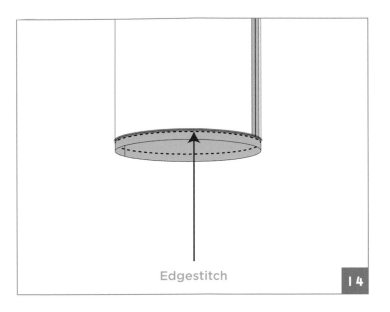

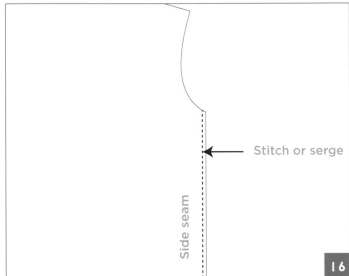

Edgestitch   **14**

Stitch or serge

Side seam

16

14. Edgestitch (page 20) close to the cut edge.

15. Repeat steps 10 to 14 for the other Sleeve. Continue with step 21.

FOR THE DRAPED VEST OPTION

16. With the right sides together, pin the Front to the Back, matching the notches. Stitch or serge. If you choose to stitch, finish the seam allowances. Repeat for the other side.

17. With the right sides together, stitch or serge the two short edges of the Arm Band (4) together, forming a loop. If you stitched the seam, press the seam allowances open; if you serged the seam, press the serged seam allowances to one side. Repeat for the other Arm Band.

18. With the wrong side inside, fold the Arm Band to create a thinner loop lengthwise. Press. Repeat for the other Arm Band.

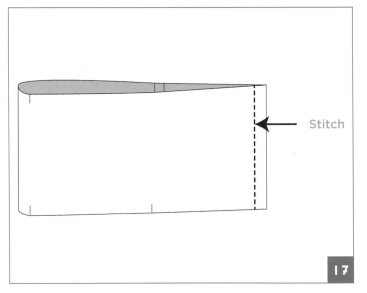

Stitch

17

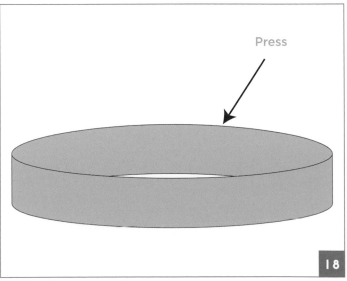

Press

18

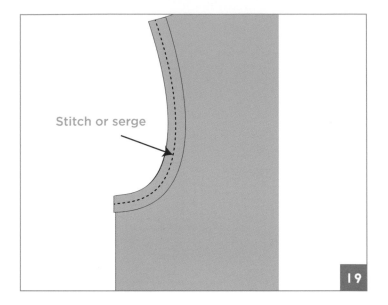

Stitch or serge

19

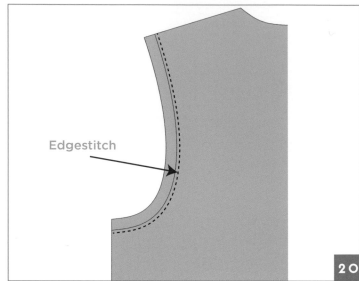

Edgestitch

20

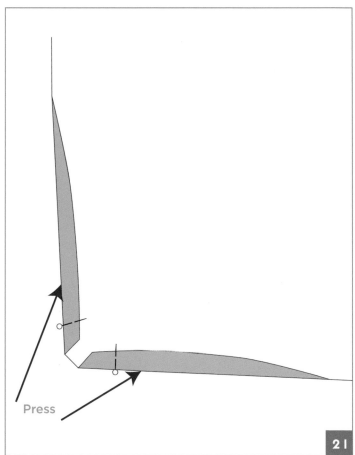

Press

21

19. Pin the Arm Band to the armhole, with the right side of the bodice against the Arm Band, matching the notches, shoulder seam, sides and raw edges. Stretch the Arm Band slightly as you pin. Stitch or serge. Press the seam allowances toward the bodice. Repeat for the other Arm Band.

20. Alternatively, edgestitch (page 20) through all the layers around the armhole. Repeat for the other Arm Band.

FOR ALL OPTIONS

21. At one of the four diagonally cut corners of the cardigan, press ½ inch (1.25 cm) of the hem toward the wrong side on both sides of the corner. Pin the fold in place.

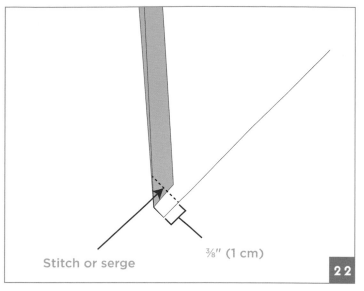

Stitch or serge   ⅜" (1 cm)   **22**

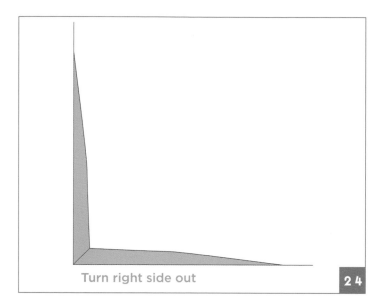

Turn right side out   **24**

2 2 . Fold the corner right sides together diagonally to align the edges. Keep the ½-inch (1.25-cm) hem folded. Stitch or serge across the short seam with a ⅜-inch (1-cm) seam allowance. The amount of seam allowance is accounted for at the side with the single fold. Stitch or serge perpendicularly from that fold.

2 3 . If you stitched the seam, trim the seam allowances and press them open. If you serged the seam, press the seam allowances to one side.

2 4 . Turn the fabric right side out.

2 5 . Repeat steps 21 to 24 for all four corners.

2 6 . For the rest of the hem (the top, sides and bottom), fold and press the hem ½ inch (1.25 cm) twice toward the wrong side. Pin. Edgestitch close to the inner fold, pivoting at the corners. Press.

2 7 . Give the cardigan or vest a good press and you are done!

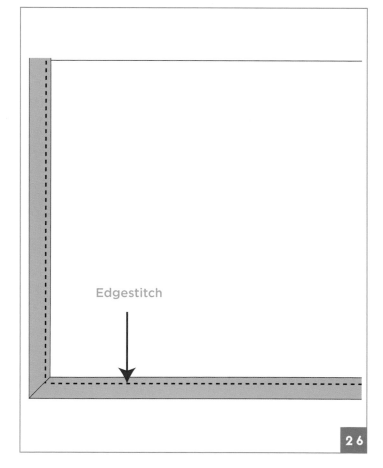

Edgestitch   **26**

THE FORTUNA

On chilly mornings, I love to wear my cozy Fortuna joggers. However, they are not just my homebound attire—I wear them out and about town too. All three options of the Fortuna—the joggers, shorts and wide-leg options—have a laid-back aesthetic combining comfort and style that is all the rage now.

The Fortuna is designed for knit fabric with good recovery. The mid-rise Fortuna has a drawstring cord in the elasticized waistband. The joggers and shorts options have slanted front pockets with a woven-fabric accent and decorative stitching at the opening, while the wide-leg option has a plain front. All options include round-bottom back pockets with a woven-fabric accent with decorative stitching.

JOGGERS
(SEE PHOTO ON PAGE 22)

FRONT   BACK

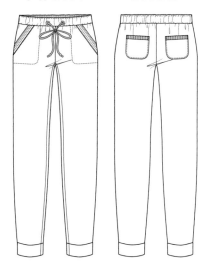

SHORTS
(SEE PHOTO ON PAGE 4)

FRONT   BACK

WIDE-LEG PANTS
(SEE PHOTO ON PAGE 78)

FRONT   BACK

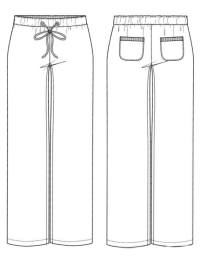

CHOOSING YOUR SIZE

1. Compare your hip circumference (the fullest part of your measured hip) to the "Body Measurements" table. Choose the size that best fits your hips. If your measurement is between sizes, choose the smaller size if you like your garment more fitted; otherwise, choose the bigger size.

2. There is no need to blend sizes from the waist to the hips on these pattern pieces. By adjusting the waist elastic, you can adjust the size of the waist.

MATERIALS

PRIMARY FABRIC
Use a medium-weight, four-way stretch knit fabric with 25 to 50 percent horizontal and vertical stretch (page 10) and good recovery. French terry, sweatshirt knit and ponte are good choices.

CONTRAST FABRIC
Use a lightweight to medium-weight woven fabric with no stretch. Quilting cotton is a good choice.

INTERFACING
Use one (1) piece of 2 x 2–inch (5 x 5–cm) lightweight woven or weft insertion fusible interfacing (page 16).

OTHER MATERIALS
Two ⅜-inch (1-cm) (inside diameter) grommets/eyelets with the corresponding tool for installation.

A piece of 1½ x 1½–inch (3.8 x 3.8–cm) lightweight, non-stretch woven fabric.

1½-inch (3.8-cm)-wide knit elastic—compare your waist circumference (the narrowest part of your waist) to the "Body Measurements" table. Then choose the elastic length based on the size that best fits your waist (see the "Elastic Requirements" table on page 80). If you are between sizes, choose the smaller size.

¼-inch (6-mm)-wide drawstring cord or ribbon as long as your waist, plus 20 inches (50 cm).

Two cord ends for the drawstring (optional).

OTHER TOOLS
A small safety pin.

BODY MEASUREMENTS

SIZE		00	0	2	4	6	8	10	12	14	16	18	20
WAIST	(IN)	25⅜	26¾	28⅛	29½	30⅞	32¼	33⅝	35	36⅜	37¾	39⅛	40½
	(CM)	64.5	68	71.5	75	78.5	82	85.5	89	92.5	96	99.5	103
HIP	(IN)	33¼	34⅝	35⅞	37¼	38⅝	40	41¼	42⅝	44	45⅜	46⅝	48
	(CM)	84.5	88	91	94.5	98	101.5	105	108	112	115.5	118.5	122

FINISHED GARMENT MEASUREMENTS

SIZE		00	0	2	4	6	8	10	12	14	16	18	20
WAIST	(IN)	28¼	29¾	31¼	32¾	34⅛	35⅝	37⅛	38⅝	40⅛	41½	43	44½
	(CM)	72	75.5	79.5	83	87	90.5	94.5	98	102	105.5	109	113
HIP	(IN)	32⅞	34⅜	35¾	37¼	38⅝	40⅛	41½	43	44⅜	45⅞	47¼	48¾
	(CM)	83.5	87.5	91	94.5	98	102	105.5	109	113	116.5	120	124
FRONT CROTCH LENGTH	(IN)	8½	8¾	8⅞	9⅛	9⅜	9½	9¾	9⅞	10⅛	10⅜	10½	10¾
	(CM)	21.5	22	22.5	23	23.5	24	24.5	25	25.5	26.5	27	27.5
BACK CROTCH LENGTH	(IN)	13¼	13⅝	13⅞	14⅛	14½	14¾	15⅛	15⅜	15¾	16	16⅜	16⅝
	(CM)	33.5	34.5	35.5	36	37	37.5	38.5	39	40	40.5	41.5	42.5
INSEAM LENGTH, JOGGERS	(IN)	30⅝	30½	30⅜	30⅛	30	29⅞	29¾	29½	29⅜	29¼	29⅛	29
	(CM)	78	77.5	77	76.5	76	76	75.5	75	74.5	74.5	74	73.5
INSEAM LENGTH, SHORTS	(IN)	3⅜	3½	3⅝	3¾	3¾	3⅞	4	4⅛	4⅛	4¼	4⅜	4½
	(CM)	8.5	9	9	9.5	9.5	10	10	10.5	10.5	11	11	11.5
INSEAM LENGTH, WIDE-LEG	(IN)	30⅝	30⅜	30¼	30⅛	30	29¾	29⅝	29½	29¼	29⅛	29	28¾
	(CM)	77.5	77	77	76.5	76	75.5	75	75	74.5	74	73.5	73

ELASTIC REQUIREMENTS

SIZE		00	0	2	4	6	8	10	12	14	16	18	20
ELASTIC LENGTH	(IN)	26⅛	27½	28⅞	30¼	31⅝	33	34⅜	35¾	37⅛	38½	39⅞	41¼
	(CM)	66.5	70	73.5	77	80.5	84	87.5	91	94.5	98	101.5	105

FABRIC REQUIREMENTS

		00	0	2	4	6	8	10	12	14	16	18	20
PRIMARY FABRIC (54 INCHES/137 CM WIDE)													
JOGGERS	(YARD)	1⅜	1⅜	1⅜	1⅝	1⅝	1⅝	2⅛	2⅛	2⅛	2⅛	2⅛	2⅛
	(CM)	125	125	125	150	150	150	195	195	195	195	195	195
SHORTS	(YARD)	⅞	⅞	⅞	⅞	⅞	⅞	1	1	1	1¼	1¼	1¼
	(CM)	80	80	80	80	80	80	90	90	90	115	115	115
WIDE-LEG	(YARD)	1½	1½	1½	2⅛	2⅛	2⅛	2⅜	2⅜	2⅜	2½	2½	2½
	(CM)	135	135	135	195	195	195	220	220	220	230	230	230
CONTRAST FABRIC (54 INCHES/137 CM WIDE)													
ALL OPTIONS	(YARD)	¼	¼	¼	¼	¼	¼	¼	¼	¼	⅜	⅜	⅜
	(CM)	30	30	30	30	30	30	30	30	30	35	35	35

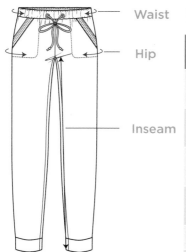

Waist
Hip
Inseam

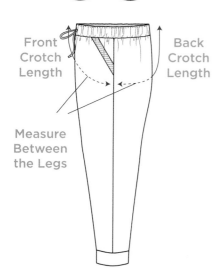

Front Crotch Length
Back Crotch Length
Measure Between the Legs

FABRIC CUTTING INSTRUCTIONS

PATTERN PIECE	FROM PRIMARY FABRIC, CUT	FROM CONTRAST FABRIC, CUT
1 - Front (Joggers or Shorts option only)	2 mirror images*	0
2 - Back (Joggers or Shorts option only)	2 mirror images*	0
3 - Front Pocket (Joggers or Shorts option only)	2 mirror images	0
4 - Cuff (Joggers option only)	2 mirror images	0
5 - Back Pocket	2 mirror images	0
6 - Waistband	1 on fold	0
7 - Front Pocket Opening (Joggers or Shorts option only)	0	2 mirror images
8 - Back Pocket Opening	0	2 mirror images
9 - Front (Wide-Leg Pants option only)	2 mirror images	0
10 - Back (Wide-Leg Pants option only)	2 mirror images	0

*Use the cut line specific for the Shorts or Joggers based on your chosen option.

LAYOUT DIAGRAMS

JOGGERS (PRIMARY FABRIC)

SIZES OO TO 2

Fold

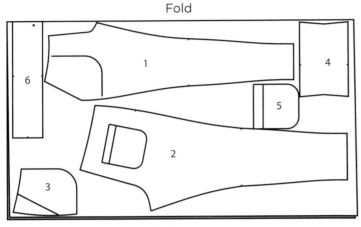

Selvage

SIZES 4 TO 8

Fold

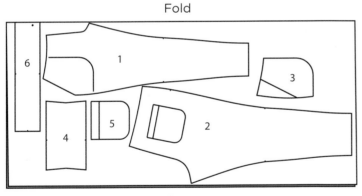

Selvage

SIZES IO TO 20

Fold

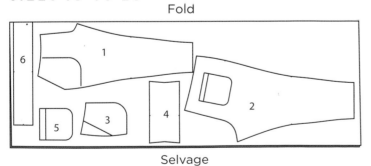

Selvage

SHORTS (PRIMARY FABRIC)

SIZES OO TO 8

Fold

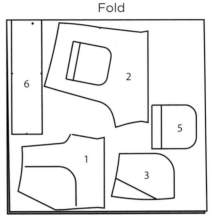

Selvage

SIZES IO TO 14

Fold

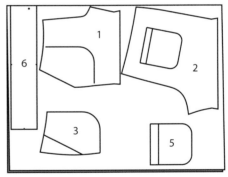

Selvage

SIZES 16 TO 20

Fold

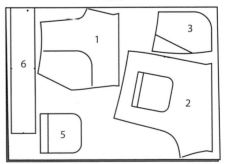

Selvage

WIDE-LEG PANTS
(PRIMARY FABRIC)

SIZES 00 TO 2

Fold

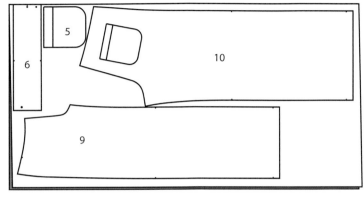

Selvage

SIZES 4 TO 14

Fold

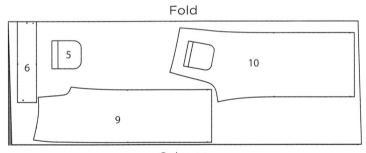

Selvage

SIZES 16 TO 20

Fold

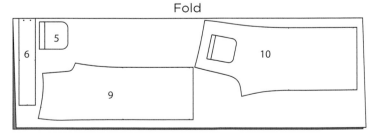

Selvage

JOGGERS OR SHORTS
(CONTRAST FABRIC)

ALL SIZES

Fold

Selvage

WIDE-LEG PANTS
(CONTRAST FABRIC)

ALL SIZES

Fold

Selvage

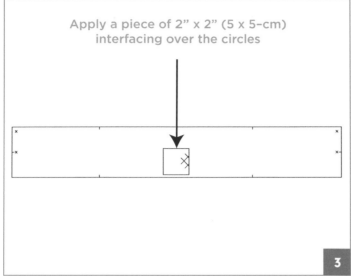

Apply a piece of 2" x 2" (5 x 5-cm) interfacing over the circles

3

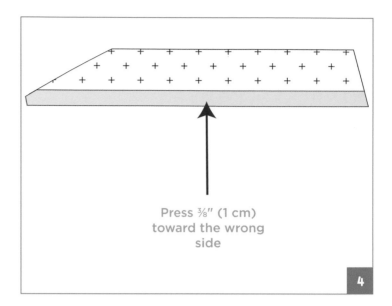

Press ⅜" (1 cm) toward the wrong side

4

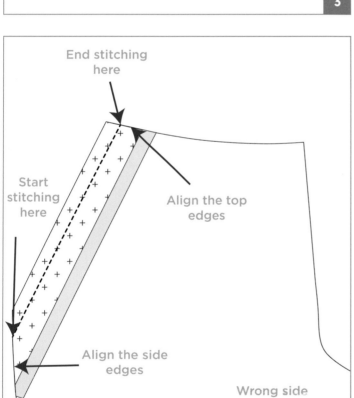

End stitching here

Start stitching here

Align the top edges

Align the side edges

Wrong side

5

SEAM ALLOWANCES

The included seam allowances are ⅜ inch (1 cm) unless stated otherwise in the process.

PROCESS

CUTTING AND MARKING FABRIC

1. Trace the pattern outlines for your size and option onto a piece of paper (see back envelope), then cut the fabric according to the Layout Diagrams (pages 82–83).

2. Transfer all the markings to the fabric before removing the pattern pieces from the fabric (pages 15–16).

STABILIZATION

3. Following the manufacturer's instructions, apply a piece of square interfacing to the wrong side of the Waistband (6) over the two circles at the center front. Re-mark the circles' positions so that you can see them in a later step.

FRONT POCKETS FOR THE JOGGERS OR SHORTS OPTIONS

Skip to step 18 for the Wide-Leg Pants option.

4. On the Front Pocket Opening (7), fold and press ⅜ inch (1 cm) of the longer edge toward the wrong side using a hot iron.

5. Pin the non-folded edge of the Front Pocket Opening to the Front (1), with the right side of the Front Pocket Opening against the wrong side of the Front, at the slanted edge, aligning the top edges and the side edges. Stitch.

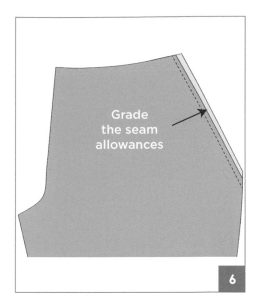

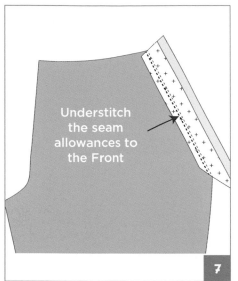

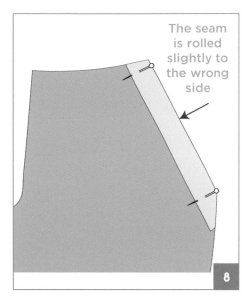

6. Grade the seam allowances (page 18); the seam allowance of the Front should be trimmed shorter than the seam allowance of the Front Pocket Opening.

7. Press the seam allowances toward the Front. Understitch (page 19) the seam allowances to the Front.

8. Turn the Front Pocket Opening to the right side of the Front. Press. The seam should slightly roll to the wrong side and is not visible from the right side. Pin the fold created in step 4 onto the Front.

9. Edgestitch (page 20) close to the fold through the Front Pocket Opening and the Front.

10. Edgestitch close to the pocket opening through all layers.

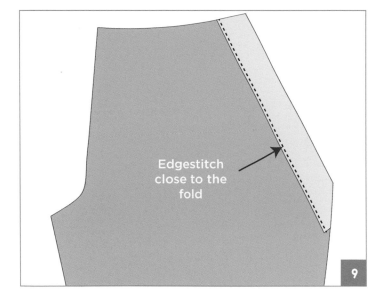

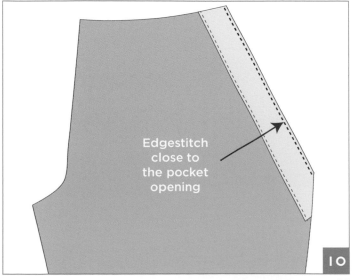

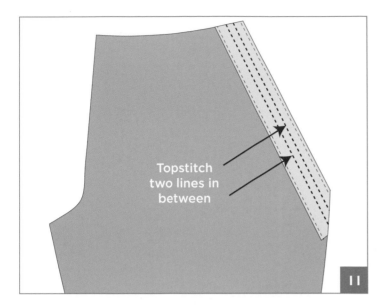

Topstitch two lines in between

11

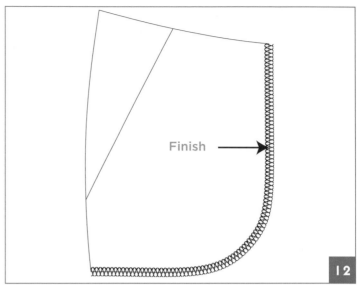

Finish

12

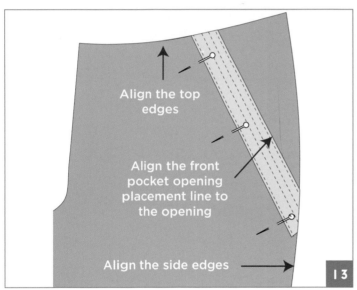

Align the top edges

Align the front pocket opening placement line to the opening

Align the side edges

13

11. Topstitch (page 20) two lines of stitching evenly between and parallel to the two lines of edgestitching. Press.

12. Finish the raw edge of the Front Pocket (3) as desired (page 18) on the straight side, through the rounded corner, to the bottom.

13. Pin the Front to the Front Pocket, with the right side of the Front Pocket against the wrong side of the Front, aligning the pocket opening to the placement line, as well as the top edges and the side edges.

14. From the wrong side, baste (page 17) close to and along the side straight edge, rounded corner and bottom straight edge of the Front Pocket through the Front.

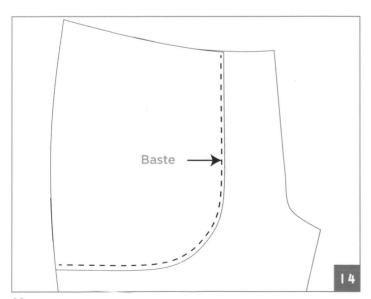

Baste

14

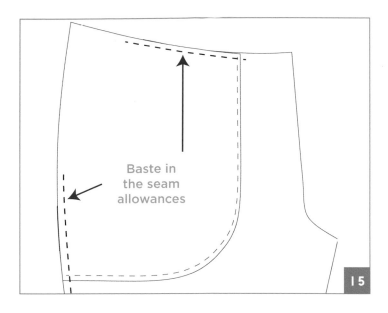

Baste in
the seam
allowances

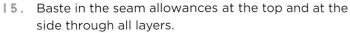

15

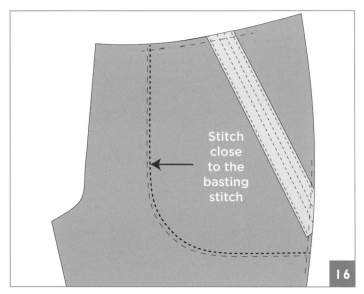

Stitch
close
to the
basting
stitch

16

15. Baste in the seam allowances at the top and at the side through all layers.

16. From the right side, stitch close to the basting stitch through the Front Pocket and the Front. Remove the line of basting stitches using your seam ripper.

17. Repeat steps 4 to 16 for the other Front Pocket Opening, Front and Front Pocket.

BACK POCKETS

18. On the Back Pocket Opening (8), fold and press ⅜ inch (1 cm) of one long edge toward the wrong side.

19. Pin the non-folded edge of the Back Pocket Opening to the Back Pocket (5), with the right side of the Back Pocket Opening against the wrong side of the Back Pocket, at the top, aligning the side edges. Stitch.

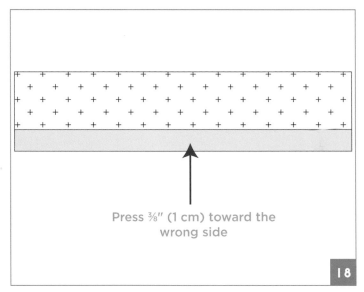

Press ⅜" (1 cm) toward the wrong side

18

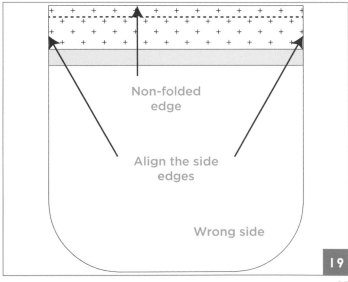

Non-folded edge

Align the side edges

Wrong side

19

Grade the seam allowances

20

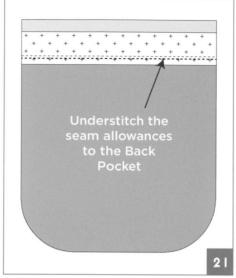

Understitch the seam allowances to the Back Pocket

21

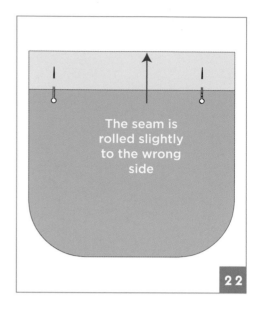

The seam is rolled slightly to the wrong side

22

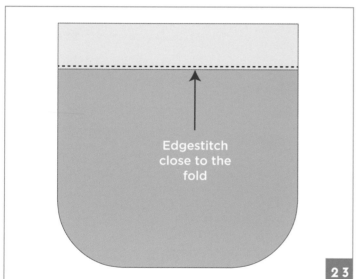

Edgestitch close to the fold

23

20. Grade the seam allowances; the seam allowance of the Back Pocket should be trimmed shorter than the seam allowance of the Back Pocket Opening.

21. Press the seam allowances toward the Back Pocket. Understitch the seam allowances to the Back Pocket.

22. Turn the Back Pocket Opening to the right side of the Back Pocket. Press. The seam should slightly roll to the wrong side and is not visible from the right side. Pin the fold created in step 18 onto the Back Pocket.

23. Edgestitch close to the fold through the Back Pocket Opening and the Back Pocket.

24. Edgestitch close to the top edge opening.

Edgestitch close to the opening

24

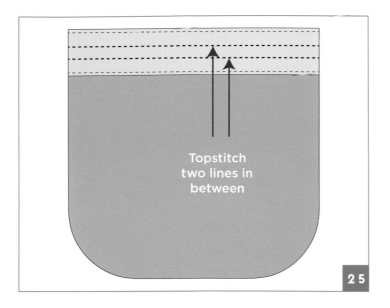

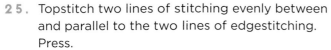

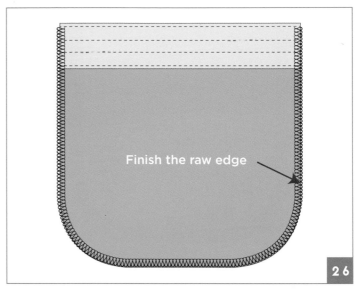

25. Topstitch two lines of stitching evenly between and parallel to the two lines of edgestitching. Press.

26. Finish the raw edge of the Back Pocket as desired.

27. Using a long stitch length of 4 mm, stitch a line in the seam allowance along the rounded corner of the Back Pocket, starting about 2 inches (5 cm) on the side to about 2 inches (5 cm) at the bottom, leaving long tails of thread at the beginning and at the end. This stitch line will be used for gathering and will make folding the seam allowance along the rounded corner easier at a later step. Repeat for the other rounded corner on the same Back Pocket.

28. Fold and press ⅜ inch (1 cm) of the side edges and bottom edge toward the wrong side.

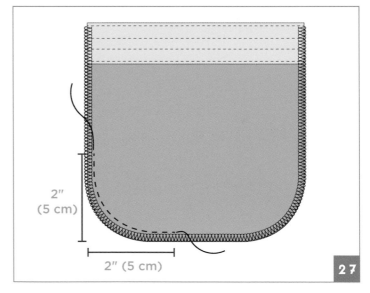

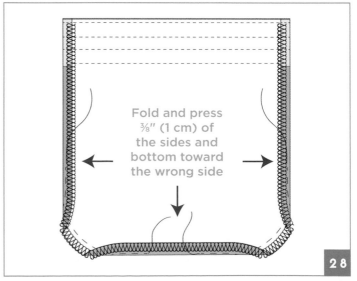

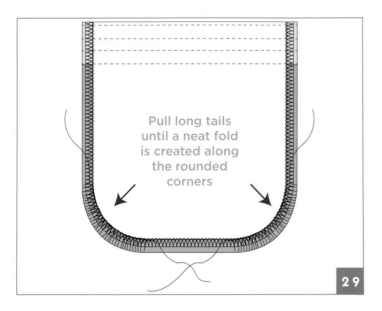

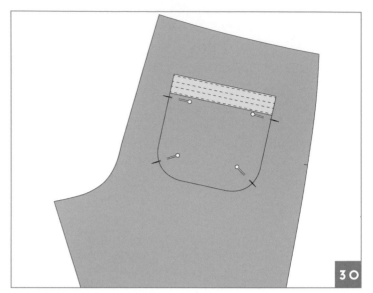

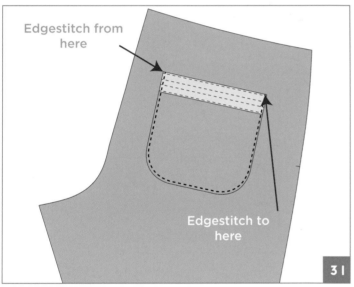

Edgestitch from here

Edgestitch to here

Pull long tails until a neat fold is created along the rounded corners

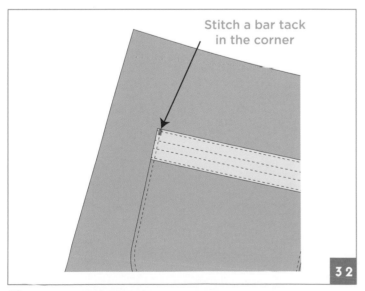

Stitch a bar tack in the corner

29. Pull the long tails of thread to gather the fabric at the rounded corner. As the fabric is gathered, a fold is created neatly around the rounded corner. Press the fold. Repeat for the other rounded corner on the same Back Pocket.

30. Pin the Back Pocket to the Back (2 or 10) according to the back pocket placement marking, with the wrong side of the Back Pocket against the right side of the Back.

31. Edgestitch the Back Pocket onto the Back from one top corner to the other top corner, around the rounded corner and edge. Leave the top opening of the pocket unstitched.

32. Stitch a bar tack in the upper corner of the Back Pocket Opening. To create a bar tack, use the zigzag stitch of your sewing machine. Use a width of 2.5 mm and a length of 0.3 mm and stitch for ¼ inch (6 mm). Stitch another bar tack in the other upper corner.

33. Repeat steps 18 to 32 for the other Back Pocket Opening, Back Pocket and Back.

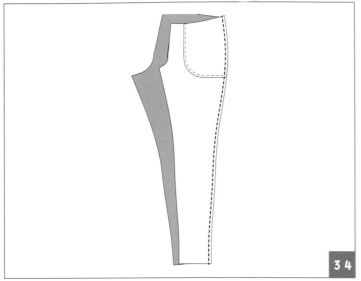

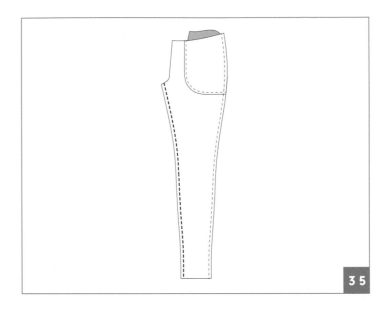

ASSEMBLE FRONT AND BACK

The same method is used for all options. The following illustrations demonstrate using the Joggers option.

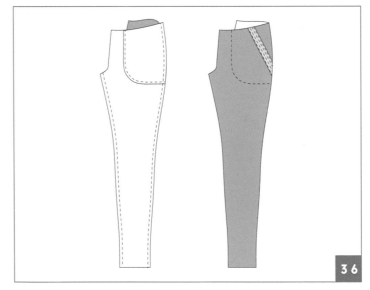

34. With the right sides together, pin the Front to the Back at the side. Stitch or serge the pinned side. Press the seam allowances toward the Back. Finish the seam allowances as desired if that seam was stitched. Repeat for the other side. Press.

35. With the right sides together, pin the Front to the Back at the inseam. Stitch or serge the pinned inseam. Press the seam allowances toward the Back. Finish the seam allowances as desired if the seam was stitched. Repeat for the other inseam. Press.

36. You now have two separate legs assembled. Turn one leg right side out and turn the other leg wrong side out.

37. Insert the right-side-out leg into the wrong-side-out leg, so that the right sides are against each other. Align the crotch edges and pin together.

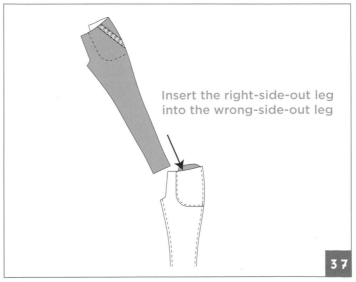

Insert the right-side-out leg into the wrong-side-out leg

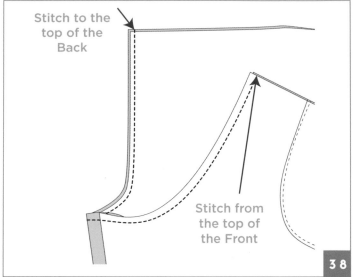

Stitch to the
top of the
Back

Stitch from
the top of
the Front

38

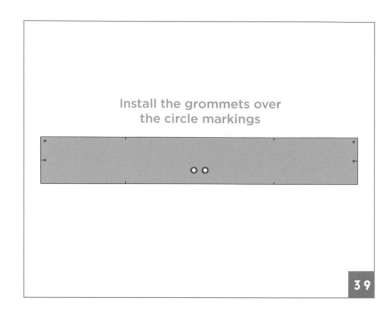

Install the grommets over
the circle markings

39

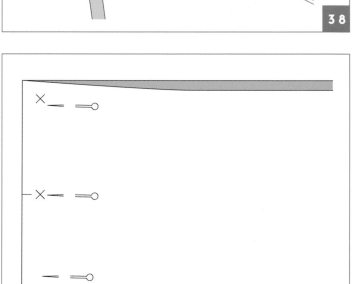

40

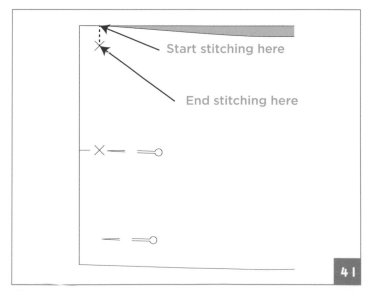

Start stitching here

End stitching here

41

38. Stitch or serge the crotch seam from the top of the Front to the top of the Back in one continuous line. Press the seam allowances toward the left-hand side as worn. Finish the seam allowances as desired if the seam was stitched. Press. Turn both legs right side out.

WAISTBAND

39. On the Waistband, over one circle marking, install a grommet according to the package's instructions. Repeat over the other circle marking.

40. With the right sides together, pin the two short ends of the Waistband together.

41. Stitch from the edge to the top cross marking.

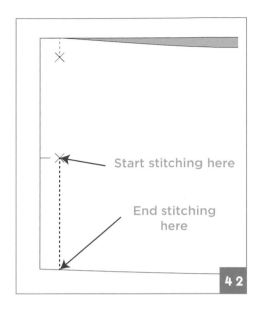

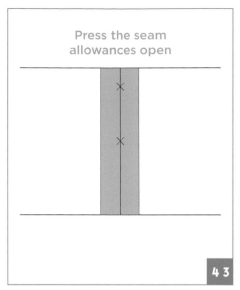

42. Stitch from the middle cross marking to the other edge. The gap left between the two crosses will be used to insert the elastic at a later step.

43. Press the seam allowances open. This seam is the center back of the Waistband.

44. With the wrong side inside, fold and press the Waistband in half lengthwise.

45. With the right sides together, pin the Waistband loop to the top edge of the assembled Front and Back, with the grommets against the right side of the Front, matching the center front and center back, as well as the notches to the side seams. The Waistband loop is slightly smaller than the top of the assembled Front and Back; therefore, you need to stretch the Waistband to match.

46. Stitch or serge around the Waistband as pinned. Finish the seam allowances as desired if the seam was stitched.

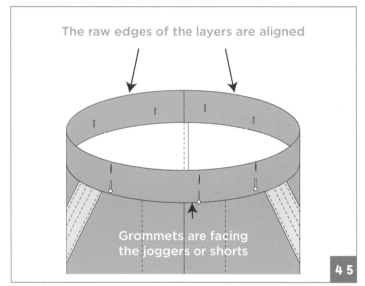

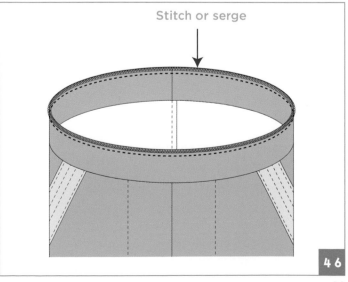

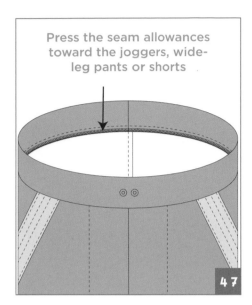

Press the seam allowances toward the joggers, wide-leg pants or shorts

47

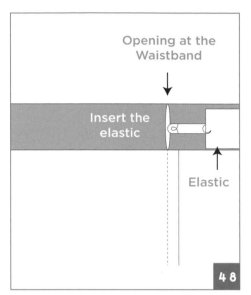

Opening at the Waistband

Insert the elastic

Elastic

48

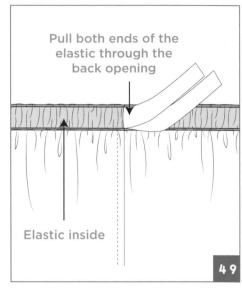

Pull both ends of the elastic through the back opening

Elastic inside

49

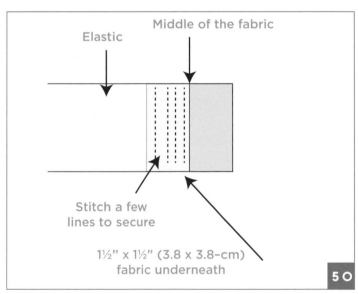

Elastic

Middle of the fabric

Stitch a few lines to secure

1½" x 1½" (3.8 x 3.8–cm) fabric underneath

50

47. Flip the Waistband up. Press the seam allowances toward the Waistband of the joggers, wide-leg pants or shorts.

48. Put a safety pin at one short end of the elastic. Thread the elastic through the center back opening of the Waistband.

49. Pull one end of the elastic through the Waistband until it emerges from the same center back opening again. Be sure not to twist the elastic inside the Waistband. Both ends of the elastic should be visible at the center back opening. The fabric of the Waistband bunches up as a result. Remove the safety pin.

50. Place the 1½ x 1½-inch (3.8 x 3.8-cm) piece of woven fabric underneath one end of the elastic. Position the elastic so that its end is in the middle of the fabric. Stitch several lines of stitches to secure the elastic onto the fabric.

51. Taking care not to twist the elastic, place the other end of the elastic onto the same piece of woven fabric. Position the elastic so that its end is in the middle of the fabric and the two ends of the elastic are butted together. Stitch several lines of stitches to secure the elastic onto the fabric.

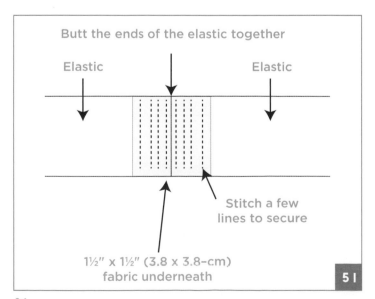

Butt the ends of the elastic together

Elastic

Elastic

Stitch a few lines to secure

1½" x 1½" (3.8 x 3.8–cm) fabric underneath

51

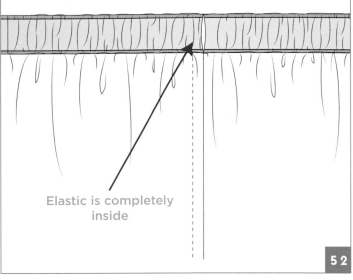

Elastic is completely inside

52

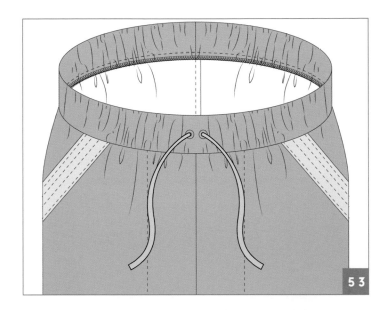

53

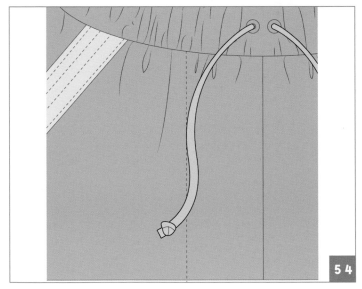

54

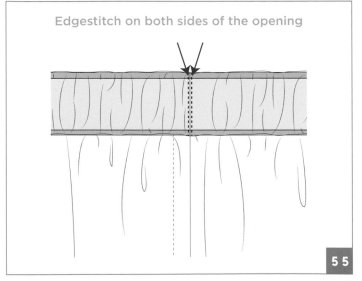

Edgestitch on both sides of the opening

55

52. Arrange the elastic so that it is completely inside the Waistband.

53. Put a safety pin at one end of the drawstring cord or ribbon. Insert the drawstring cord or ribbon into one of the grommet holes. Thread it through the Waistband until it comes out of the other grommet hole. If your safety pin is too large for the grommet hole, wrap one end of the drawstring in a few layers of cellophane tape to make it rigid. Then you can insert the end through the Waistband.

54. If you are using cord ends, apply them at the end of the drawstring cord or ribbon. Otherwise, tie a knot at each end of the drawstring cord or ribbon.

55. Make sure the drawstring cord or ribbon is centered. Arrange the center back opening of the Waistband so that very little, if any, of the elastic is visible. Edgestitch along each side of the opening on the Waistband through all layers, including the elastic.

56. Evenly distribute the fabric of the Waistband along the elastic.

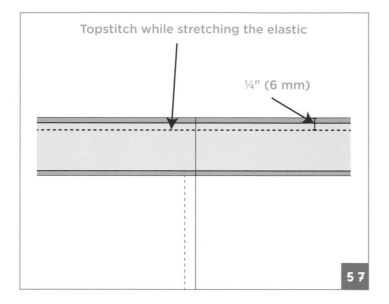

Topstitch while stretching the elastic

¼" (6 mm)

57

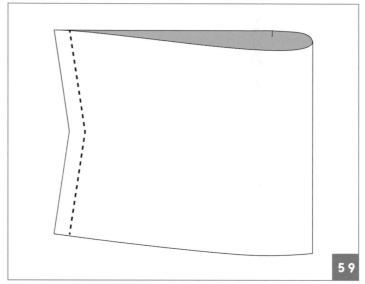

59

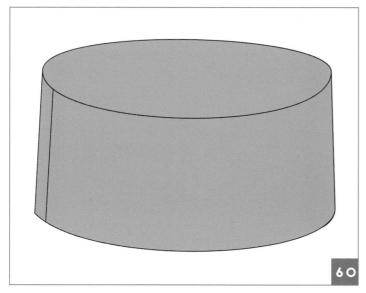

60

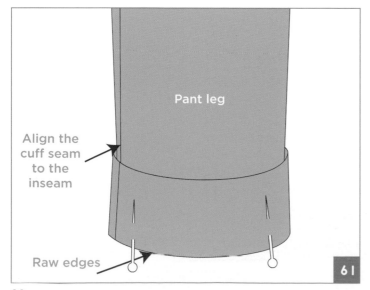

Pant leg

Align the cuff seam to the inseam

Raw edges

61

57. Starting at the center back seam, using a stitch length of 3 mm, topstitch the circumference of the Waistband through the elastic while stretching the elastic fully. Be careful to not catch the drawstring in your topstitching. The topstitch line is ¼ inch (6 mm) from the top edge of the waistband.

58. Steam the waistband with your steam iron so that the elastic shrinks to its original length.

JOGGERS
Skip to step 65 for the Shorts or Wide-Leg Pants option.

59. With the right side inside, pin and stitch the bent edges of the Cuff (4) together, forming a loop. Press the seam allowances open.

60. With the wrong side inside, roll down one raw edge to meet the other to form a cuff.

61. Slip the bottom of the leg inside the Cuff, with the right side of the leg against the Cuff, matching the raw edges. Pin. The seam of the Cuff should be matching the inseam of the leg. The Cuff is slightly smaller than the leg opening; stretch the Cuff as you pin the layers together.

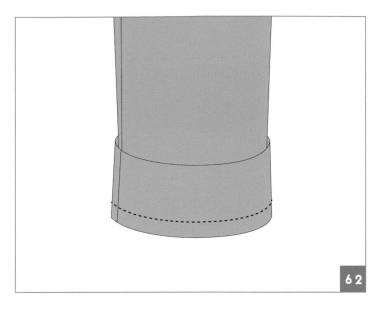

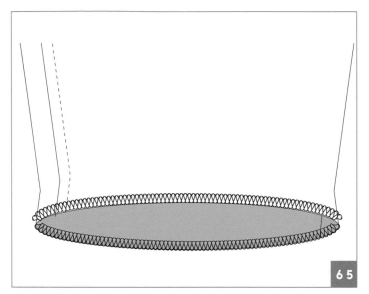

62. Stitch or serge the pinned seam. Press the seam allowance toward the leg. Finish the seam allowances as desired if the seam was stitched.

63. Repeat steps 59 to 62 for the other Cuff and leg.

64. Skip to the Finishing section below.

SHORTS OR WIDE-LEG PANTS

The same method is used for the Shorts and Wide-Leg Pants options. The following illustrations demonstrate using the Shorts option.

65. Finish the bottom edge of the leg as desired. Repeat for the other leg.

66. Fold and press 1 inch (2.5 cm) of the bottom edge of the leg toward the wrong side. Pin.

67. Topstitch around the shorts' leg ⅞ inch (2.2 cm) from the fold. Press.

FINISHING

68. Give the Joggers, Shorts or Wide-Leg Pants a good press and you are done!

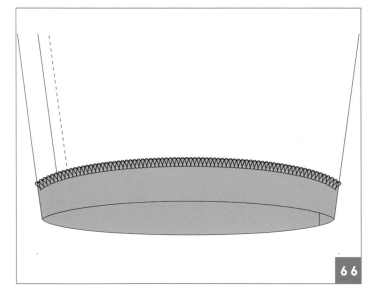

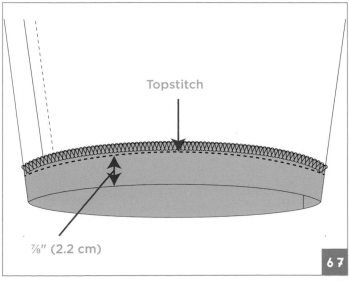

Topstitch

⅞" (2.2 cm)

THE CASTLEPOINT

I like wrap skirts, especially ones with curved lines. The curved lines elongate the legs and add interest to a garment. However, one downside is that I never feel secure in a wrap skirt. I feel that at any moment, the wind could blow my skirt completely open. Enter the faux-wrap skirt! You get to have the look of a wrap skirt without the insecurity.

The Castlepoint Faux-Wrap Skirt is a pull-on straight skirt with a petal-shaped front. Only the back waistband has elastic, so the front looks just like a regular skirt. Another feature I love is the feminine and stylish hi-lo hem. The Castlepoint Faux-Wrap Skirt comes in a long option and a short option. The skirt even comes with in-seam pockets!

The waistband of the Castlepoint sits at the narrowest point of your waist. It is semi-fitted from the waist to the hips, and then the skirt falls straight down from the hips. Your left knee is designed to be visible at the highest point of the overlap.

FAUX-WRAP LONG SKIRT
(SEE PHOTO ON PAGE 98)

FRONT · BACK

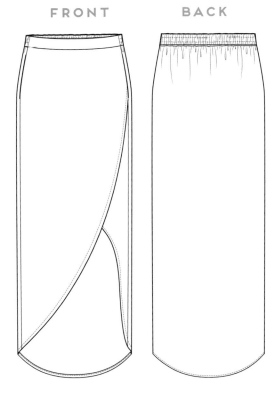

FAUX-WRAP SHORT SKIRT
(SEE PHOTO ON PAGE 22)

FRONT · BACK

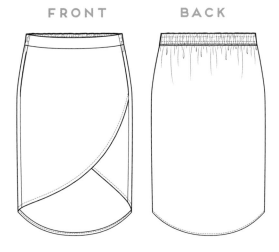

CHOOSING YOUR SIZE

1. Compare your hip circumference (the fullest part of your measured hip) to the "Body Measurements" table. Choose the size that best fits your hips. If your measurement is between sizes, choose the smaller size if you like your garment more fitted; otherwise, choose the bigger size.

2. There is no need to blend sizes from the waist to the hips on these pattern pieces. By adjusting the waist elastic, you can adjust the size of the waist. In fact, if you blend to a smaller size for your waist, you will not be able to pull the skirt up past your hips.

MATERIALS

PRIMARY FABRIC

Use a lightweight to medium-weight woven fabric. Linen, crepe, rayon challis, poplin and tropical wool are good choices. Both the right side and wrong side of the fabric will be visible when the skirt is worn, so choose your fabric accordingly.

INTERFACING

Use lightweight to medium-weight fusible woven or weft insertion interfacing (page 16).

OTHER MATERIALS

24 inches (61 cm) of ⅜-inch (1-cm)-wide straight fusible stay tape (page 16); you can also make your own using lightweight woven fusible interfacing cut on the straight grain.

1½-inch (3.8-cm)-wide knit elastic—compare your waist circumference (the narrowest part of your waist) to the "Body Measurements" table (page 100). Choose the elastic length based on the size that best fits your waist (see the "Elastic Requirements" table on page 100). If you are between sizes, choose the smaller size.

OTHER TOOLS

A small safety pin.

BODY MEASUREMENTS

SIZE		OO	O	2	4	6	8	10	12	14	16	18	20
HIP	(IN)	33¼	34⅝	35⅞	37¼	38⅝	40	41¼	42⅝	44	45⅜	46⅝	48
	(CM)	84.5	88	91	94.5	98	101.5	105	108	112	115.5	118.5	122

FINISHED GARMENT MEASUREMENTS

SIZE		OO	O	2	4	6	8	10	12	14	16	18	20
HIP	(IN)	33⅞	35⅜	36⅞	38⅜	40	41½	43	44½	46	47½	49⅛	50⅝
	(CM)	86	90	94	97.5	101.5	105.5	109	113	117	121	124.5	128.5
LONG SKIRT, BACK LENGTH	(IN)	36⅞	36⅞	36⅞	36⅞	36⅞	36⅞	36⅞	36⅞	36⅞	36⅞	36⅞	36⅞
	(CM)	94	94	94	94	94	94	94	94	94	94	94	94
SHORT SKIRT, BACK LENGTH	(IN)	23	23	23	23	23	23	23	23	23½	24	24½	25
	(CM)	58.5	58.5	58.5	58.5	58.5	58.5	58.5	58.5	59.5	61	62	63.5

FABRIC REQUIREMENTS

		OO	O	2	4	6	8	10	12	14	16	18	20
PRIMARY FABRIC (54 INCHES/137 CM WIDE)													
LONG SKIRT	(YARD)	1⅝	1⅝	1⅝	1¾	1¾	1¾	1¾	1¾	1¾	1⅞	1⅞	1⅞
	(CM)	150	150	150	160	160	160	160	160	160	170	170	170
SHORT SKIRT	(YARD)	1⅛	1⅛	1⅛	1⅜	1⅜	1⅜	1⅜	1⅜	1⅜	1½	1½	1½
	(CM)	100	100	100	125	125	125	125	125	125	135	135	135
INTERFACING (20 INCHES/51 CM WIDE)													
ALL OPTIONS	(YARD)	⅝	⅝	⅝	⅝	⅝	⅝	⅝	⅝	¾	¾	¾	¾
	(CM)	60	60	60	60	60	60	60	60	70	70	70	70

ELASTIC REQUIREMENTS

	OO	O	2	4	6	8	10	12	14	16	18	20
(IN)	9¾	10¼	11	11⅝	12¼	12⅞	13½	14	14⅝	15¼	15⅞	16⅜
(CM)	25	26	28	29.5	31	32.5	34.5	35.5	37	38.5	40.5	41.5

FABRIC CUTTING INSTRUCTIONS

PATTERN PIECE	FROM PRIMARY FABRIC, CUT	FROM INTERFACING, CUT
1 - Right Front (overlap)	1*/**	0
2 - Left Front (underlap)	1*/**	0
3 - Back	1 on fold*	0
4 - Pocket	2 sets of 2 mirror images	0
5 - Front Waistband	1 on fold	1 on fold
6 - Back Waistband	1 on fold	0

*Use the short hem marked "Cut Here for the Short Option" for the short option, and use the longer hem marked "Cut Here for the Long Option" for the long option.
**When cutting the piece, the right sides of the fabric and the pattern piece should be facing upward.

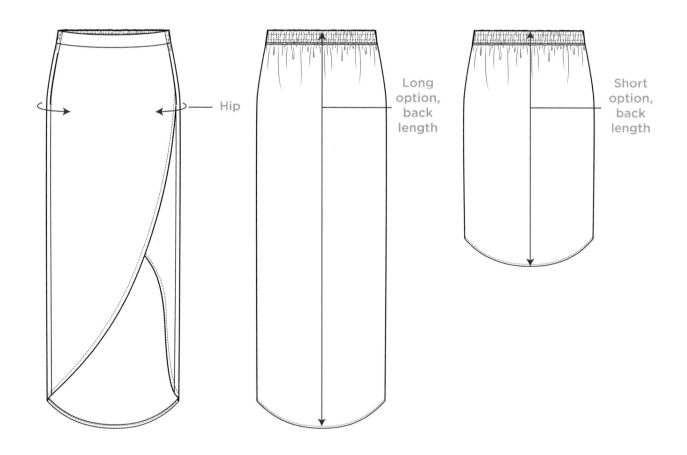

Hip

Long option, back length

Short option, back length

LAYOUT DIAGRAMS

LONG SKIRT (PRIMARY FABRIC)

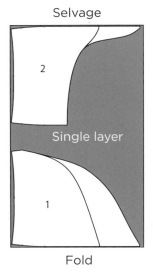

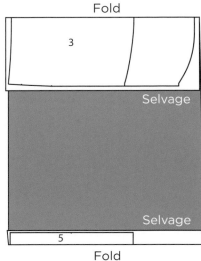

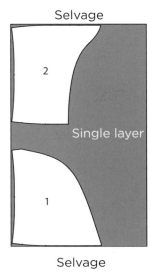

Re-fold the remaining fabric to cut the remaining pieces:

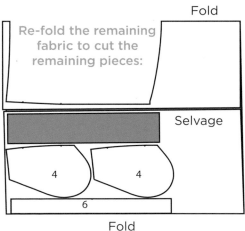

SHORT SKIRT (PRIMARY FABRIC)

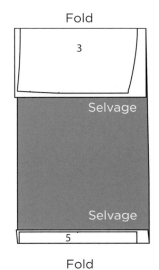

Re-fold the remaining fabric to cut the remaining pieces:

ALL OPTIONS (INTERFACING)

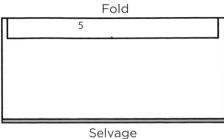

Fold

5

Selvage

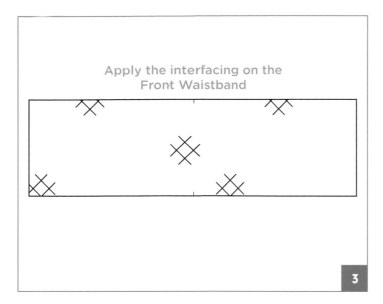

Apply the interfacing on the Front Waistband

3

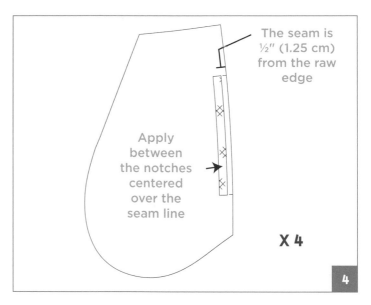

The seam is ½" (1.25 cm) from the raw edge

Apply between the notches centered over the seam line

X 4

4

SEAM ALLOWANCES

The included seam allowances are ½ inch (1.25 cm) unless stated otherwise in the process.

PROCESS

The same method is used for both the long option and the short option. The short option is used for the illustrations.

CUTTING AND MARKING FABRIC

1. Trace the pattern outlines for your size and option onto a piece of paper (see back envelope), then cut the fabric according to the Layout Diagrams (page 102).

2. Transfer all the markings to the fabric before removing the pattern pieces from the fabric (pages 15–16).

STABILIZATION

3. Following the manufacturer's instructions, apply the interfacing to the wrong side of the Front Waistband (5).

4. Cut a piece of 6-inch (15.25-cm)-long fusible stay tape. Using a hot iron, apply the fusible stay tape centered over the seam line on the wrong side of the Pocket (4) between the notches. The seam line is ½ inch (1.25 cm) from the cut edge. Repeat for the three other Pocket pieces.

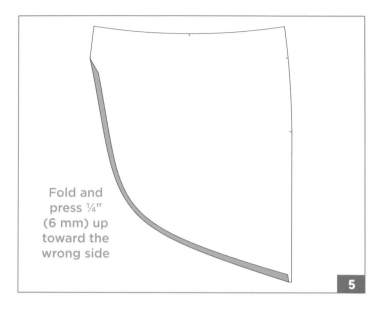

Fold and press ¼" (6 mm) up toward the wrong side

5

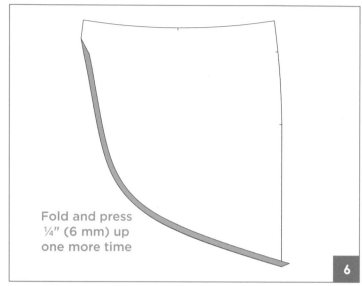

Fold and press ¼" (6 mm) up one more time

6

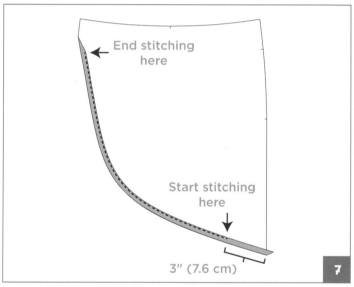

End stitching here

Start stitching here

3" (7.6 cm)

7

FRONT

5. On the Right Front (1), fold and press ¼ inch (6 mm) of the bottom edge toward the wrong side using a hot iron.

6. Fold and press ¼ inch (6 mm) of the bottom edge toward the wrong side again.

7. Note that one side of the Right Front is longer than the other side. Starting in 3 inches (7.6 cm) from the longer side, edgestitch (page 20) close to and along the first fold. Stitch all the way toward the shorter side of the Right Front. Be sure not to stretch the fabric while stitching.

8. On the Left Front (2), fold and press ¼ inch (6 mm) of the bottom edge toward the wrong side. The curve on the long option is different, but the same method is used.

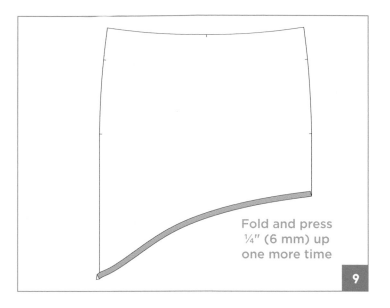

Fold and press ¼" (6 mm) up one more time

9

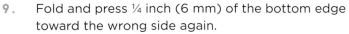

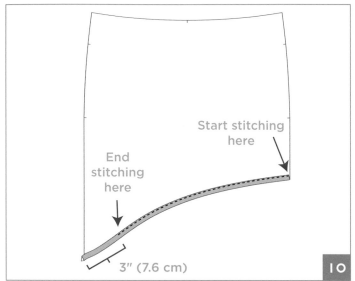

Start stitching here

End stitching here

3" (7.6 cm)

10

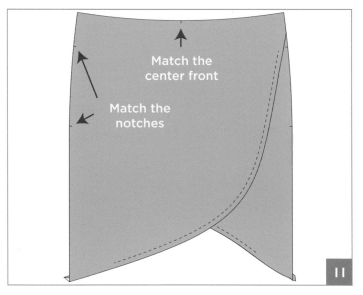

Match the center front

Match the notches

11

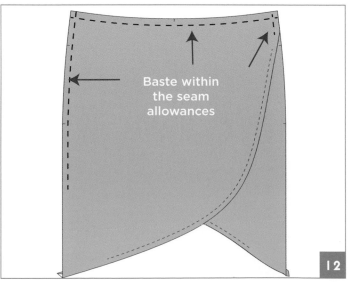

Baste within the seam allowances

12

9. Fold and press ¼ inch (6 mm) of the bottom edge toward the wrong side again.

10. Note that one side of the Left Front is longer than the other side. Starting at the shorter side, edgestitch close to and along the first fold. Stitch toward the longer side, but stop stitching 3 inches (7.6 cm) before reaching the longer side. Be sure not to stretch the fabric while stitching.

11. Lay the Left Front wrong side down on your table, so that the right side is facing up. Lay the Right Front wrong side down on top of the Left Front, matching the center fronts and the side notches.

12. Pin and baste (page 17) the two layers together at the sides and at the top within the seam allowances.

13. This two-layered, assembled skirt front will be treated as one piece and referred to as the Front Skirt in the following steps.

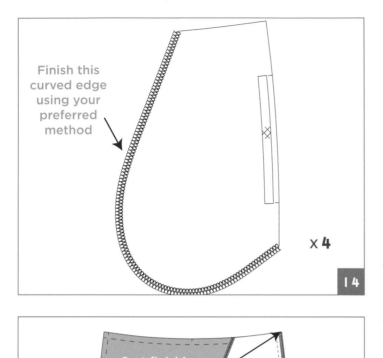

Finish this curved edge using your preferred method

x 4

14

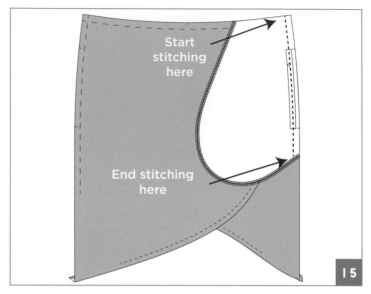

Start stitching here

End stitching here

15

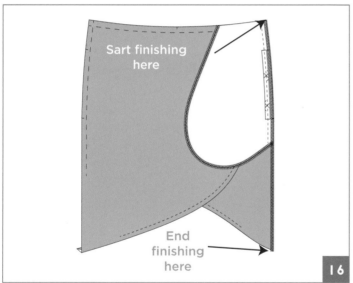

Sart finishing here

End finishing here

16

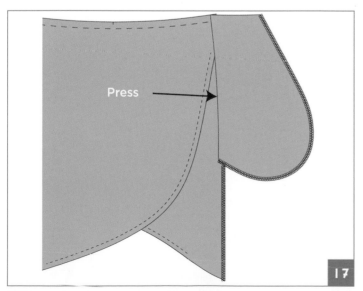

Press

17

POCKET

14. For all four Pocket (4) pieces, finish the curved edges as desired (page 18). Trim as little of the fabric as possible if you are serging the edges, so that the seam allowance remains accurate when you stitch the seam.

15. With the right sides together, pin one Pocket piece to the Front Skirt, matching the notches. Stitch.

16. Finish the raw edges of the layers together from the top to the bottom of the Front Skirt. Mark the notches again so you can still see them later.

17. Press the seam allowances toward the Pocket.

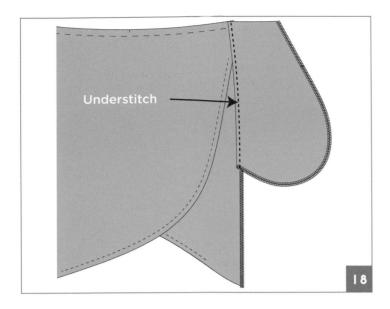

Understitch

`18`

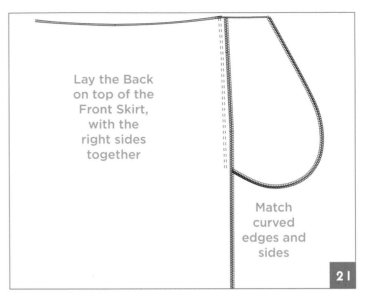

Lay the Back on top of the Front Skirt, with the right sides together

Match curved edges and sides

`21`

18. Understitch (page 19) the seam allowances to the Pocket.

19. Repeat steps 15 to 18 for the other side of the Front Skirt.

20. Repeat steps 15 to 18 for both sides of the Back (3).

21. With the right sides together and the Pocket piece extended, pin the Back to the Front Skirt and the Pocket pieces together, matching the curved edges of the Pocket and the side.

22. Stitch the curved edges of the Pocket together.

23. Stitch another line in the seam allowance ¼ inch (6 mm) from the first line.

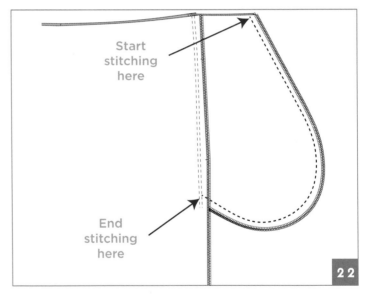

Start stitching here

End stitching here

`22`

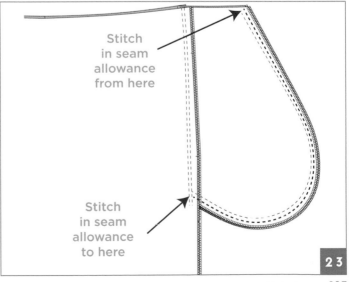

Stitch in seam allowance from here

Stitch in seam allowance to here

`23`

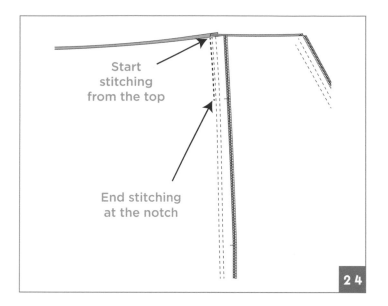

Start stitching from the top

End stitching at the notch

24

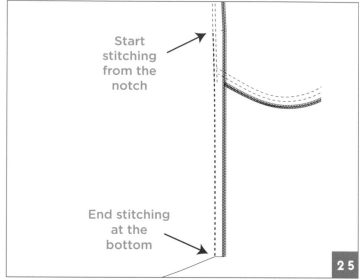

Start stitching from the notch

End stitching at the bottom

25

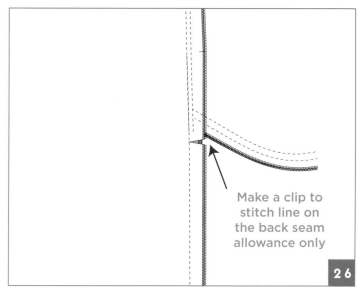

Make a clip to stitch line on the back seam allowance only

26

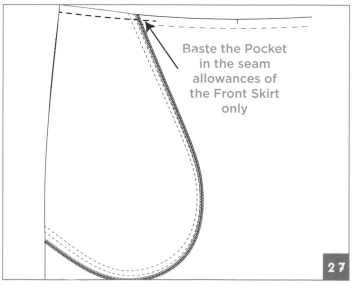

Baste the Pocket in the seam allowances of the Front Skirt only

27

24. With the Pocket pieces out of the way, stitch from the top of the skirt to the first pocket notch. At the notch, stitch back and forth to reinforce. Make sure that this stitch line is slightly on the left side of the previous pocket stitch line.

25. At the second notch, stitch back and forth to reinforce, and continue to stitch from the second notch to the bottom of the skirt. The bottom of the skirt is unfolded. Make sure that this stitch line is slightly on the left side of the previous pocket stitch line.

26. Using your scissors, make a small clip in the back seam allowance below the Pocket. Do not cut through the stitch line. Press the side seam allowances above the clip toward the Front Skirt, and press the side seam allowances below the clip open.

27. Baste the top of the Pocket to the top of the Front Skirt. Repeat for the other Pocket.

28. Repeat steps 21 to 27 to make the other Pocket for the other side of the skirt.

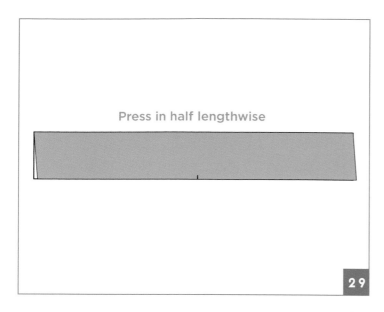

Press in half lengthwise

29

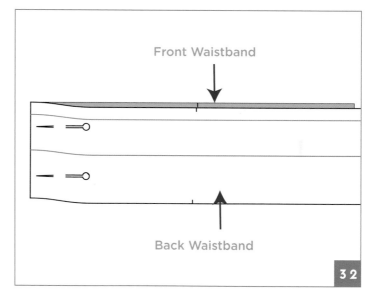

Press ½″ (1.25 cm)
toward the wrong side

30

Front Waistband

Back Waistband

32

WAISTBAND

29. With the wrong side inside, press the Front Waistband in half lengthwise to create a middle crease.

30. Open the Front Waistband again. Fold and press ½ inch (1.25 cm) of one long edge toward the wrong side. Be careful not to erase the middle crease created in the previous step.

31. Repeat steps 29 and 30 for the Back Waistband (6).

32. Temporarily unfold the Back Waistband and the Front Waistband. With the right sides together, pin the Back Waistband to the Front Waistband at one of the short ends.

33. Stitch from the edge to the ½-inch (1.25-cm) crease made in step 30.

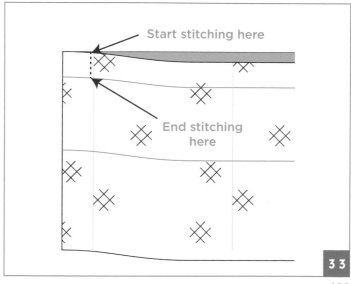

Start stitching here

End stitching here

33

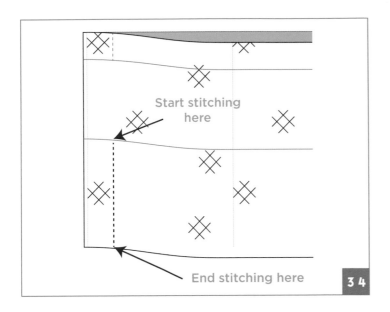

Start stitching here

End stitching here

34

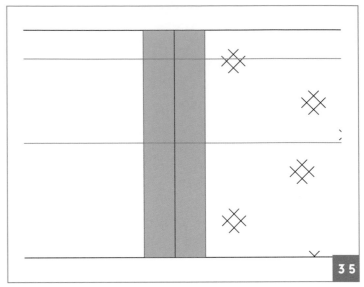

35

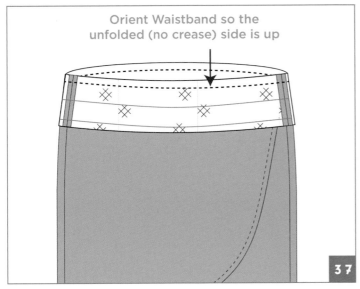

Orient Waistband so the unfolded (no crease) side is up

37

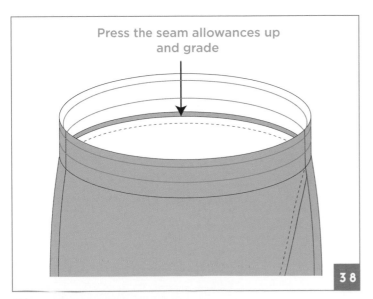

Press the seam allowances up and grade

38

34. Stitch from the middle crease made in step 29 to the bottom edge. The gap left between the stitch lines will be used for inserting the elastic later.

35. Press the seam allowances open, taking care not to erase the creases created in steps 29 and 30.

36. Repeat steps 32 to 35 to stitch the other short ends of the Front Waistband and Back Waistband together. Now you have a Waistband Loop.

37. With the right sides together, pin the unfolded side (the side with no crease) of the Waistband Loop to the top edge of the skirt, matching the side seams, center front and center back of the Waistband Loop to the skirt. Stitch around the waist as pinned.

38. Press the seam allowances toward the Waistband. Grade the seam allowances (page 18) with the Waistband's seam allowance trimmed shorter.

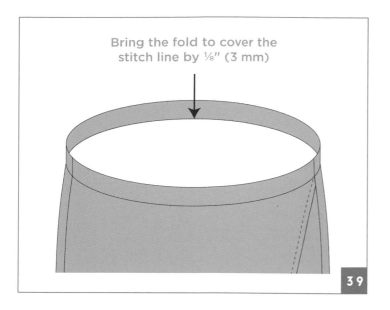

Bring the fold to cover the stitch line by ⅛" (3 mm)

39

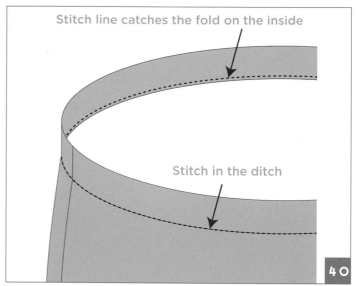

Stitch line catches the fold on the inside

Stitch in the ditch

40

39. Bring the fold made in step 30 to meet the stitch line of the Waistband. The fold should slightly cover the stitch line by ⅛ inch (3 mm). Pin and baste in place.

40. From the right side, stitch in the ditch (page 20) in the waist seam, catching the fold on the wrong side.

41. Put a safety pin at one short end of the elastic. Thread the entire elastic through the side opening of the Waistband into the Back Waistband.

42. Arrange the elastic so that ½ inch (1.25 cm) of it extends into the Front Waistband. The fabric of the Back Waistband will bunch up. Pin the elastic through the Back Waistband close to the side openings to hold it in place. You can carefully try on the skirt. If the elastic is too loose, you can shorten it accordingly. Remove the safety pin.

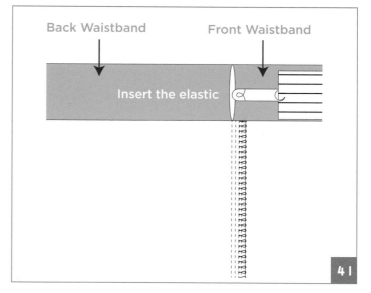

Back Waistband   Front Waistband

Insert the elastic

41

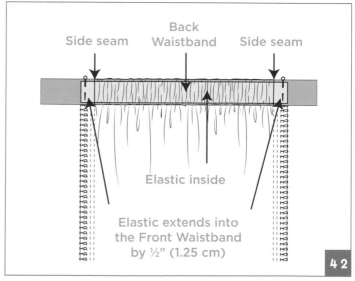

Side seam   Back Waistband   Side seam

Elastic inside

Elastic extends into the Front Waistband by ½" (1.25 cm)

42

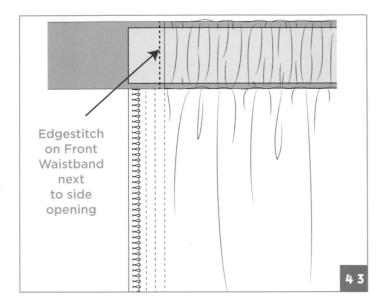

Edgestitch
on Front
Waistband
next
to side
opening

43

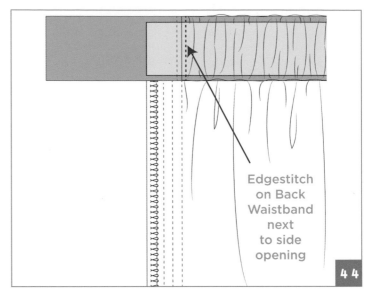

Edgestitch
on Back
Waistband
next
to side
opening

44

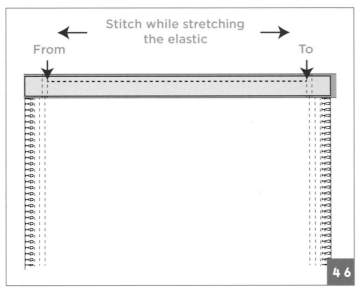

Stitch while stretching
the elastic

← From   To →

46

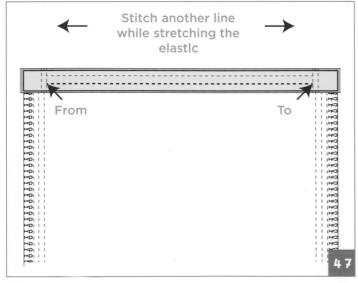

Stitch another line
while stretching the
elastic

← From   To →

47

43. Arrange the side opening so that very little, if any, of the elastic is visible. Edgestitch along the opening on the Front Waistband through all layers. Repeat the edgestitch on the other side.

44. Edgestitch along the opening on the Back Waistband through all layers. Repeat the edgestitch on the other side.

45. Evenly distribute the fabric of the Back Waistband along the elastic.

46. Starting at one side seam, using a stitch length of 3 mm, topstitch (page 20) the elastic while stretching the elastic fully until you reach the other side seam. Make sure you use both hands, one in front of the feed dog (the metal teeth beneath your presser foot) and one behind the feed dog, to stretch the elastic so that you do not pull the needle while stitching. The topstitch line is ⅝ inch (1.6 cm) from the top edge of the waistband.

47. Topstitch another line ⅝ inch (1.6 cm) below the first topstitch line using the same method.

48. Steam the Waistband with your steam iron so that the elastic shrinks to its original length.

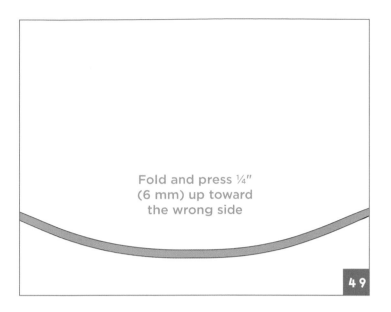

Fold and press ¼"
(6 mm) up toward
the wrong side

49

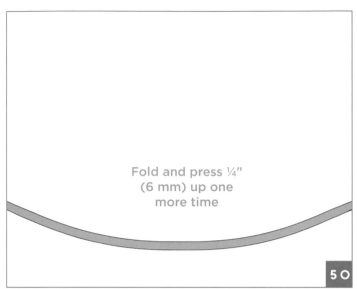

Fold and press ¼"
(6 mm) up one
more time

50

FINISHING

49. On the Back, fold and press ¼ inch (6 mm) of the bottom edge toward the wrong side.

50. Fold and press ¼ inch (6 mm) of the bottom edge toward the wrong side again.

51. Re-fold the bottom edges of the Left Front and Right Front that you left unstitched in steps 6 and 9. Press.

52. Starting where the stitch line was left off on the Left Front (step 10), edgestitch close to and along the first fold. Stitch from the Left Front, through the Back, to the Right Front, where the stitch line was left off (step 7). Be sure not to stretch the fabric while stitching.

53. Give the skirt a good press and you are done!

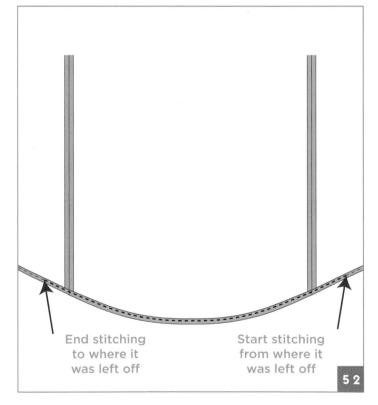

End stitching
to where it
was left off

Start stitching
from where it
was left off

52

THE PALERMO

I think of the Palermo as an all-seasons dress or top. It is elegant yet modern. In my mind, you can wear the Palermo with boots and a sweater in the fall or winter, or you can wear it with sandals and a pair of dramatic earrings in the spring or summer.

The Palermo has a center front seam split at the top. The neckline is elasticized to create a gathered look, and the seven-eighth-length raglan sleeves are also elasticized at the hem. The Palermo dress has a separate sash, but you are welcome to change it out with a statement belt.

The Palermo comes in both a dress option and a top option. The dress option includes a two-tiered gathered skirt that falls slightly below the knee as well as a removable sash, whereas the top option has a straight hem at the hip. Both the top and dress options are designed to have a relaxed fit.

PEASANT BLOUSE
(SEE PHOTO ON PAGE 6)

FRONT

BACK

TIERED DRESS
(SEE PHOTO ON PAGE 114)

FRONT

BACK

CHOOSING YOUR SIZE

1. Compare your bust circumference (the fullest part of your measured bust) to the "Body Measurements" table. Choose the size that best fits your bust. If your measurement is between sizes, choose the smaller size if you like your garment more fitted; otherwise, choose the bigger size.

2. Compare your hip circumference (the fullest part of your measured hip) to the "Body Measurements" table. Choose the size that best fits your hips. If your measurement is between sizes, choose the smaller size if you like your garment more fitted; otherwise, choose the bigger size.

3. If you have different sizes for the bust and hip, you can blend sizes (page 11). The waist is designed to be very relaxed, and you do not have to consider the waist when selecting a size.

MATERIALS

PRIMARY FABRIC
Use a lightweight and soft woven fabric with no stretch. Double gauze, crepe and lawn cotton are good choices.

OTHER MATERIALS
⅜-inch (1-cm)-wide knit elastic for the neckline. For lengths, see the "Elastic Requirements" table on page 116.

22 inches (56 cm) of ⅜-inch (1-cm)-wide knit elastic for the sleeve hem.

OTHER TOOLS
A small safety pin.

BODY MEASUREMENTS

SIZE		OO	O	2	4	6	8	10	12	14	16	18	20
BUST	(IN)	31⅛	32½	33⅞	35⅛	36½	37⅞	39¼	40⅝	42	43¼	44⅝	46
	(CM)	79	82.5	86	89	92.5	96	99.5	103	106.5	110	113.5	117
HIP	(IN)	33¼	34⅝	35⅞	37¼	38⅝	40	41¼	42⅝	44	45⅜	46⅝	48
	(CM)	84.5	88	91	94.5	98	101.5	105	108	112	115	118.5	122

FINISHED GARMENT MEASUREMENTS

SIZE		OO	O	2	4	6	8	10	12	14	16	18	20
BUST	(IN)	37⅛	38⅝	40⅛	41⅝	43⅛	44¾	46¼	47¾	49¼	50¾	52¼	53¾
	(CM)	94.5	98	102	106	109.5	113.5	117.5	121	125	129	132.5	136.5
WAIST	(IN)	35½	37	38½	40	41½	43	44½	46	47½	49	50½	52
	(CM)	90	94	98	101.5	105.5	109	113	117	120.5	124.5	128.5	132
HIP	(IN)	39⅛	40⅝	42⅛	43⅝	45⅛	46¾	48¼	49¾	51¼	52¾	54¼	55¾
	(CM)	99.5	103	107	111	115	118.5	122.5	126.5	130	134	138	141.5

FABRIC REQUIREMENTS

		OO	O	2	4	6	8	10	12	14	16	18	20
PRIMARY FABRIC (54 INCHES/137 CM WIDE)													
PEASANT BLOUSE	(YARD)	1⅜	1⅜	1⅜	1½	1½	1½	1¾	1¾	1¾	2	2	2
	(CM)	125	125	125	135	135	135	160	160	160	180	180	180
TIERED DRESS	(YARD)	2⅝	2⅝	2⅝	3	3	3	3⅛	3⅛	3⅛	3¼	3¼	3¼
	(CM)	240	240	240	275	275	275	285	285	285	300	300	300

ELASTIC REQUIREMENTS

	OO	O	2	4	6	8	10	12	14	16	18	20
(IN)	23⅝	24	24⅜	24¾	25¼	25⅝	26	26⅜	26¾	27⅛	27½	28
(CM)	60	61	62	63	64	65	66	67	68	69	70	71

FABRIC CUTTING INSTRUCTIONS

PATTERN PIECE	FROM PRIMARY FABRIC, CUT
1 - Front	2 mirror images
2 - Back	1 on fold
3 - Sleeve	2 mirror images
4 - Skirt Top Ruffle (for the Tiered Dress option only)	2 on fold
5 - Skirt Bottom Ruffle (for the Tiered Dress option only)	2 on fold
6 - Sash (for the Tiered Dress option only)	2
7 - Neck Bias Tape	1

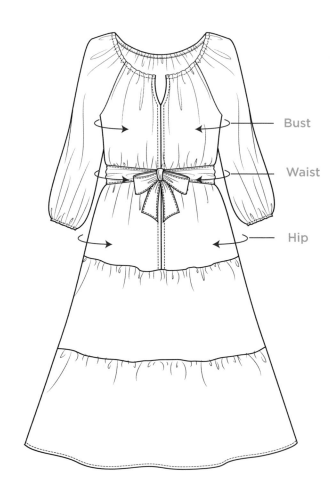

Bust

Waist

Hip

LAYOUT DIAGRAMS

PEASANT BLOUSE

SIZES 00 TO 8

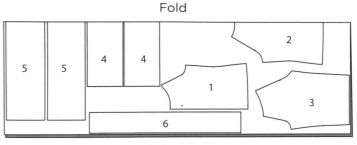

Fold

2

1

3

Selvage

Open up the remaining fabric to cut the remaining piece:

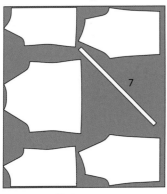

Selvage

7

Selvage

SIZES 10 TO 20

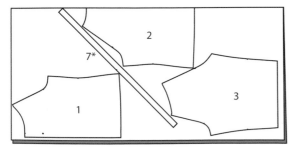

Fold

2

7*

1

3

Selvage

TIERED DRESS

SIZES 00 TO 2

Fold

5 5 4 4 2

1

3

6

Selvage

Open up the remaining fabric to cut the remaining piece:

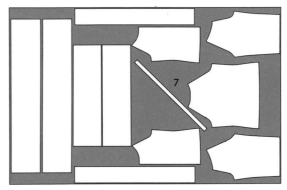

Selvage

7

Selvage

SIZES 4 TO 20

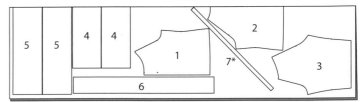

Fold

5 5 4 4 2

1 7*

3

6

Selvage

*Only one piece will be used

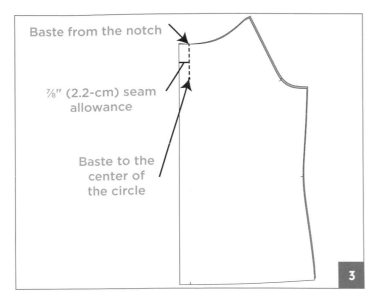

Baste from the notch

⅞" (2.2-cm) seam allowance

Baste to the center of the circle

3

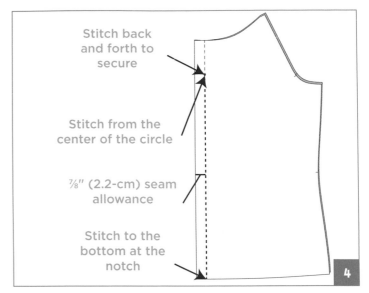

Stitch back and forth to secure

Stitch from the center of the circle

⅞" (2.2-cm) seam allowance

Stitch to the bottom at the notch

4

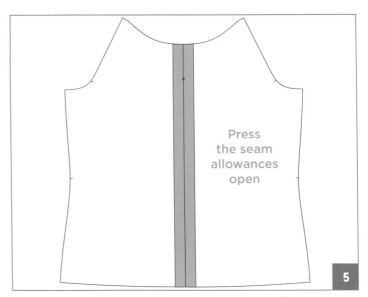

Press the seam allowances open

5

Tuck ⅜" (1 cm) of the seam allowances under and press

6

SEAM ALLOWANCES

The included seam allowances are ½ inch (1.25 cm) unless stated otherwise in the process.

PROCESS

CUTTING AND MARKING FABRIC

1. Trace the pattern outlines for your size and option onto a piece of paper (see back envelope). Then cut the fabric according to the Layout Diagrams (page 118).

2. Transfer all the markings to the fabric before removing the pattern pieces from the fabric (pages 15–16).

FRONT

3. With the right sides together, pin the two Front (1) pieces together at the center front. Baste (page 17) with a seam allowance of ⅞ inch (2.2 cm) from the top notch to the center of the circle.

4. Stitch back and forth at the center of the circle, then continue to stitch straight down to the bottom notch. The seam allowance is ⅞ inch (2.2 cm).

5. Using a hot iron, press the seam allowances open.

6. Tuck ⅜ inch (1 cm) of the seam allowance under on both sides. Press.

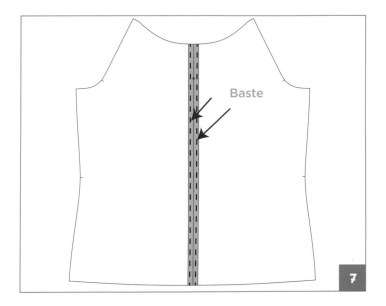

Baste

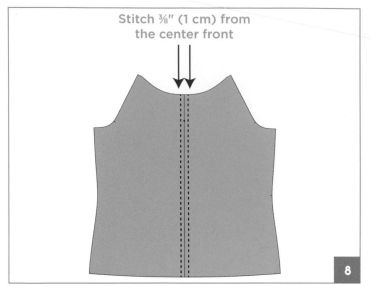

Stitch ⅜" (1 cm) from
the center front

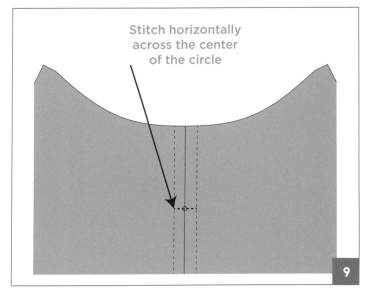

Stitch horizontally
across the center
of the circle

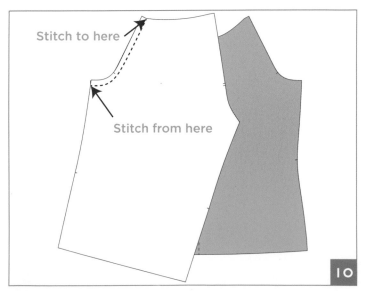

Stitch to here

Stitch from here

7. Baste the folds in place.

8. From the right side, topstitch (page 20) ⅜ inch
(1 cm) away from the center seam starting at the
top to the bottom. Repeat on the other side of the
center seam. Remove the lines of basting stitch
made in step 7.

9. At the same level as the circle, stitch horizontally
from one topstitch line to the other topstitch line,
through the center of the circle.

RAGLAN SLEEVES

10. With the right sides together, pin the Sleeve (3)
to the Front, matching the single notches. Stitch.
Press the seam allowances toward the Sleeve.
Finish the seam allowances as desired (page 18).
Repeat for the other side of the Front and the
other Sleeve.

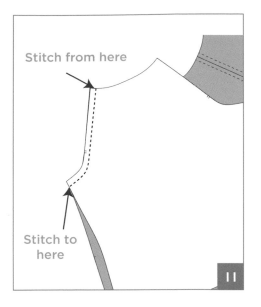

Stitch from here

Stitch to here

11

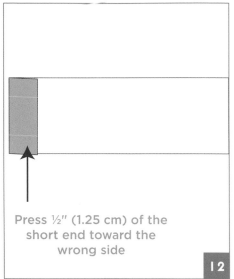

Press ½" (1.25 cm) of the short end toward the wrong side

12

Fold in half lengthwise and press

13

11. With the right sides together, pin the Back (2) to the Sleeve, matching the double notches. Stitch. Press the seam allowances toward the Sleeve. Finish the seam allowances as desired. Repeat for the other side of the Back and the other Sleeve.

NECKLINE

12. Fold and press ½ inch (1.25 cm) of the short end of the Neck Bias Tape (7) toward the wrong side. Repeat for the other short end.

13. With the wrong side inside, fold the Neck Bias Tape in half lengthwise and press to create a middle crease.

14. Open the Neck Bias Tape. With the wrong side inside, bring one long raw edge to the middle crease and press.

15. Bring the other long raw edge to the middle crease and press. The middle crease will not be used anymore; only the two side creases will be used in the following steps.

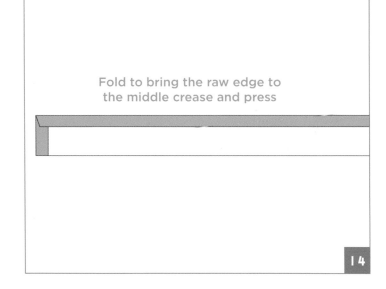

Fold to bring the raw edge to the middle crease and press

14

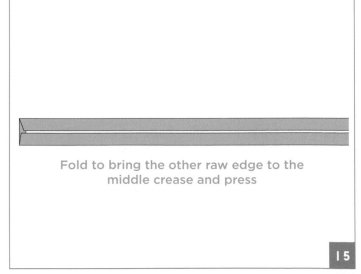

Fold to bring the other raw edge to the middle crease and press

15

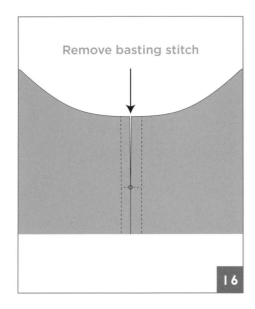

Remove basting stitch

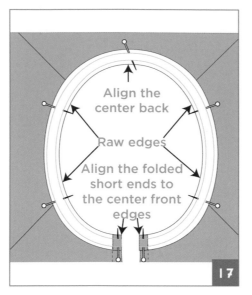

Align the center back

Raw edges

Align the folded short ends to the center front edges

17

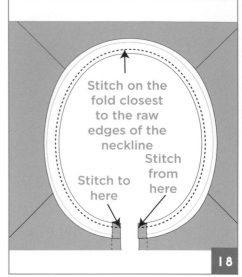

Stitch on the fold closest to the raw edges of the neckline

Stitch from here

Stitch to here

18

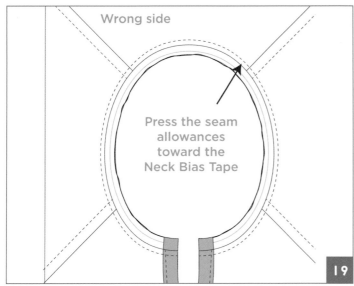

Wrong side

Press the seam allowances toward the Neck Bias Tape

19

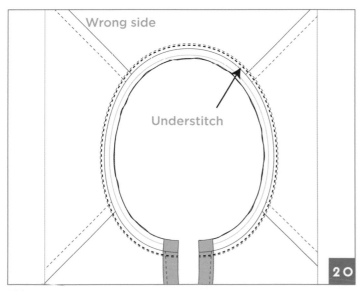

Wrong side

Understitch

20

16. Remove the basting stitch at the center front of the Front above the circle.

17. Open up the folds created in steps 14 and 15, but do not unfold the short ends. With the right sides together, pin one long raw edge of the Neck Bias Tape to the raw edge of the neckline—start by pinning one folded short end to the center front, then, without twisting the tape, pin the notch of the Neck Bias Tape to the center back, and finally, pin the other folded short end to the opposite side of the center front. Now you can pin the rest of the Neck Bias Tape between those alignment points to the neckline.

18. Stitch along the fold closest to the raw edge of the neckline through both layers.

19. Press the seam allowances toward the Neck Bias Tape. Grade the seam allowances (page 18); the Neck Bias Tape's seam allowance should be trimmed shorter.

20. Understitch (page 19) the seam allowances to the Neck Bias Tape.

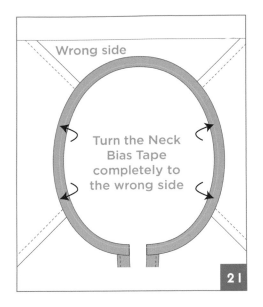

Wrong side

Turn the Neck Bias Tape completely to the wrong side

21

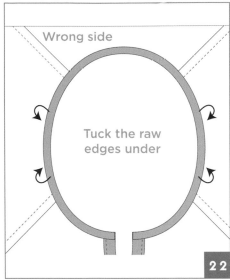

Wrong side

Tuck the raw edges under

22

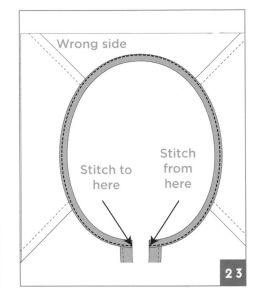

Wrong side

Stitch to here

Stitch from here

23

21. Turn the Neck Bias Tape completely toward the wrong side of the garment, so that the Neck Bias Tape is not visible from the right side of the garment.

22. Tuck the raw edge of the Neck Bias Tape under using the crease that is now the closest to the raw edge. Press.

23. Stitch along the fold through all layers. This results in a channel that will be used as the elastic casing. To ensure a flat neckline, do not straighten the neckline while stitching the fabric; keep the layers flat and turn the fabric at the curves. Press the neckline.

24. Put a safety pin at one short end of the neckline elastic. Thread the elastic through one center front opening of the neckline.

25. Arrange the neckline elastic so that the ends are at each side of the center front. The fabric around the neckline gathers up as a result. Remove the safety pin.

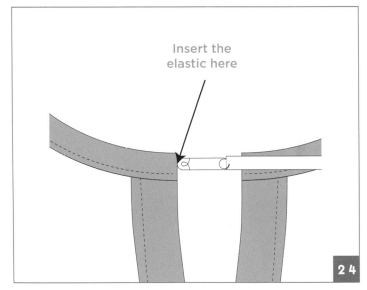

Insert the elastic here

24

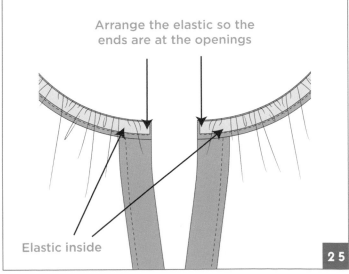

Arrange the elastic so the ends are at the openings

Elastic inside

25

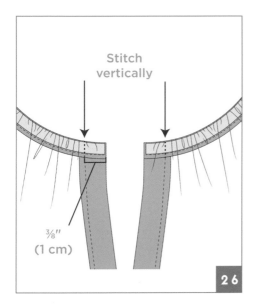

Stitch vertically

⅜″ (1 cm)

`26`

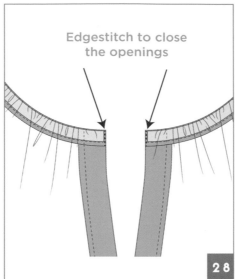

Edgestitch to close the openings

`28`

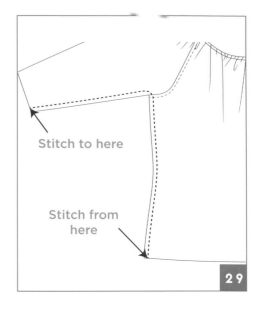

Stitch to here

Stitch from here

`29`

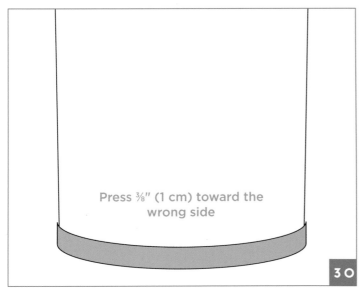

Press ⅜″ (1 cm) toward the wrong side

`30`

26. Stitch vertically ⅜ inch (1 cm) from the center front over the casing and through the elastic. This stitch line connects to the topstitching made in step 8. Repeat for the other side of the center front.

27. If any of the elastic is visible at the openings, trim them back a little. Take care not to cut the fabric.

28. Edgestitch (page 20) vertically to close the elastic casing opening. Repeat for the other side of the center front.

SIDE

29. With the right sides together, pin the Front to the Back, matching notches and underarm seams. Stitch from the bottom edge of the Front and Back to the bottom edge of the Sleeve. Press the seam allowances open. Finish the seam allowances as desired. Repeat for the other side.

SLEEVE ELASTIC

30. Fold and press ⅜ inch (1 cm) of the bottom edge of the Sleeve toward the wrong side.

31. Fold and press ½ inch (1.25 cm) toward the wrong side again.

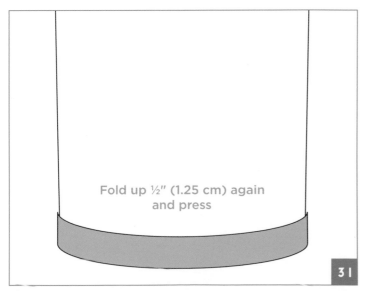

Fold up ½″ (1.25 cm) again and press

`31`

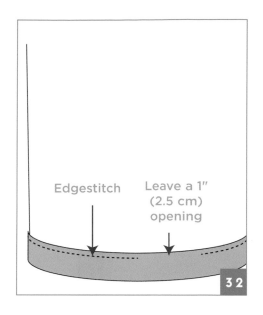

Edgestitch

Leave a 1″ (2.5 cm) opening

32

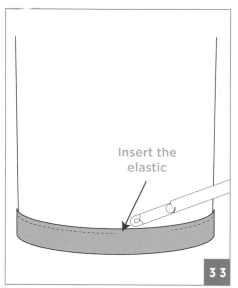

Insert the elastic

33

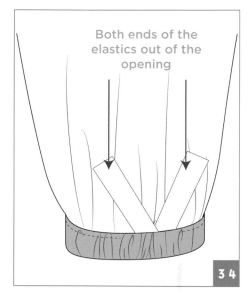

Both ends of the elastics out of the opening

34

32. Edgestitch close to the first fold, but leave an opening of about 1 inch (2.5 cm).

33. Cut the sleeve hem elastic in half so you have 11 inches (28 cm) of the elastic for one sleeve hem. Put a safety pin at one short end of the sleeve hem elastic. Thread the elastic through the unstitched opening.

34. Pull the elastic through until both ends of the elastic are visible at the unstitched opening. Be sure not to twist the elastic inside the sleeve hem channel. The fabric around the sleeve hem gathers up as a result. Remove the safety pin.

35. Overlap the ends of the elastic by ½ inch (1.25 cm) and put a safety pin through the layers to temporarily secure. Try on the garment and adjust the sleeve hem elastic according to your preference.

36. When you are happy with the circumference of the sleeve hem, remove the safety pin and stitch a few lines over the ends of the elastic to secure. Cut off the excess elastic if you have any.

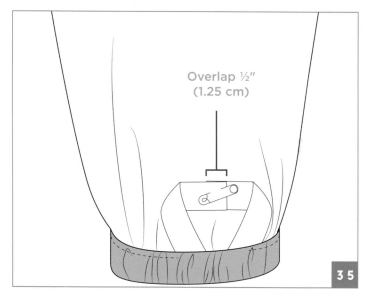

Overlap ½″ (1.25 cm)

35

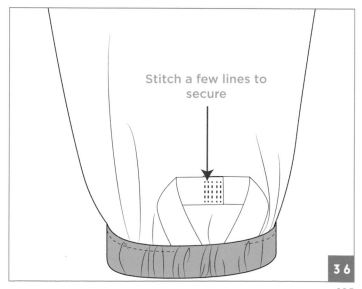

Stitch a few lines to secure

36

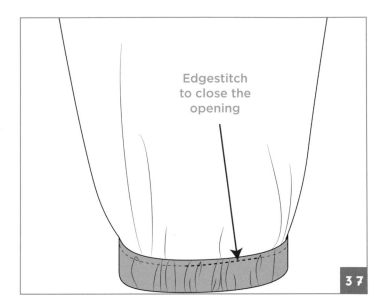

Edgestitch
to close the
opening

37

39

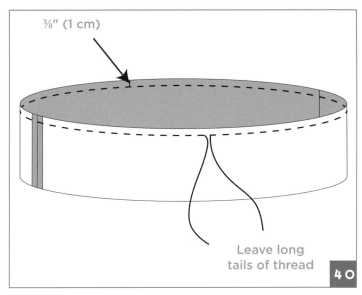

⅜" (1 cm)

Leave long
tails of thread

40

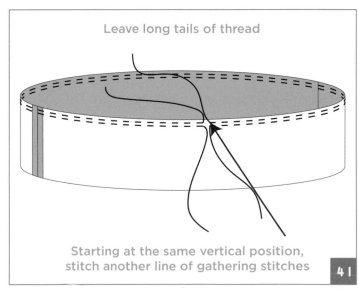

Leave long tails of thread

Starting at the same vertical position,
stitch another line of gathering stitches

41

37. Arrange the elastic so that it is completely inside
the sleeve hem channel. Edgestitch close to the
fold to close up the opening.

38. Repeat steps 30 to 37 for the other Sleeve.

SKIRT (FOR THE DRESS OPTION ONLY)
Skip to step 53 for completing the Blouse option.

39. With the right sides together, pin the short ends
of two Skirt Top Ruffle (4) pieces together. Stitch.
Press the seam allowances open. Finish the seam
allowances as desired. Repeat for the other short
ends of the same Skirt Top Ruffle pieces to create
a loop.

40. Using a long stitch length of 4 mm, stitch along
one long edge of the assembled Skirt Top Ruffle,
leaving long tails of thread at the beginning and
the end. This stitch line is ⅜ inch (1 cm) from the
raw edge.

41. Starting at the same vertical position, stitch
another line with a long stitch length (4 mm)
between the first line and the raw edge, taking
care not to stitch on the first line. Similarly, leave
long tails of thread at the beginning and the end.

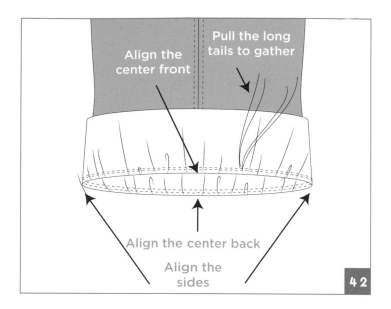

Align the center front

Pull the long tails to gather

Align the center back

Align the sides

42

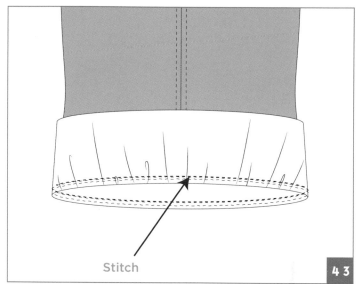

Stitch

43

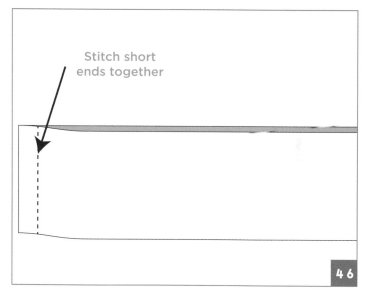

Stitch short ends together

46

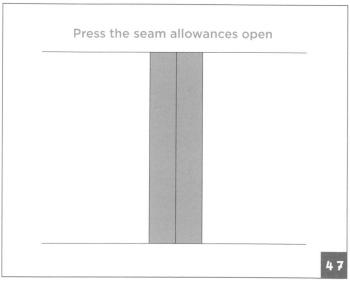

Press the seam allowances open

47

42. With the right sides together, pin the assembled Skirt Top Ruffle (the side with the two stitch lines) to the bottom of the bodice at the side seams, center front and center back. Pull the long tails of the gathering stitches to gather the fabric, so that the circumference of the assembled Skirt Top Ruffle is the same as the bottom of the bodice. Put in a few more pins to secure the gathered fabric to the bodice.

43. Stitch the layers together as pinned.

44. Press the seam allowances toward the bodice. Finish the seam as desired.

45. Repeat steps 39 to 44 for the Skirt Bottom Ruffle (5), sewing it to the bottom of the assembled Skirt Top Ruffle.

SASH

46. With the right sides together, pin the short ends of the two Sash (6) pieces together. Stitch.

47. Press the seam allowances open.

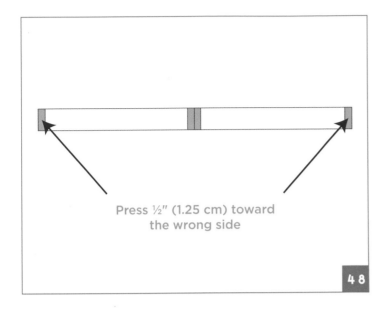

Press ½" (1.25 cm) toward
the wrong side

48

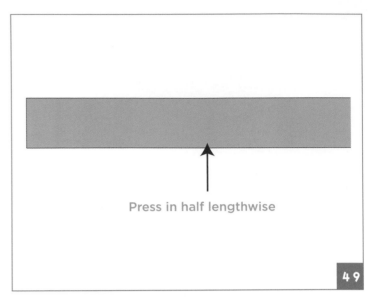

Press in half lengthwise

49

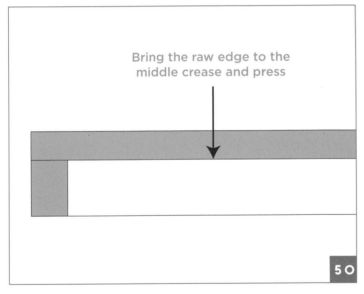

Bring the raw edge to the
middle crease and press

50

48. Press ½ inch (1.25 cm) of the short end toward the
wrong side. Repeat for the other short end.

49. With the wrong side inside, fold and press the
Sash in half lengthwise to create a middle crease.

50. Open the Sash at the middle crease. With the
wrong side inside, bring one long raw edge to the
middle crease and press.

51. Bring the other long raw edge to the middle
crease and press.

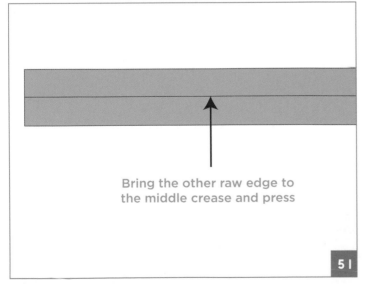

Bring the other raw edge to
the middle crease and press

51

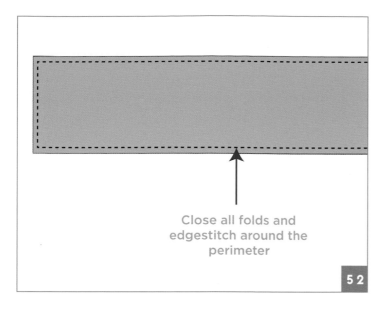

Close all folds and
edgestitch around the
perimeter

52

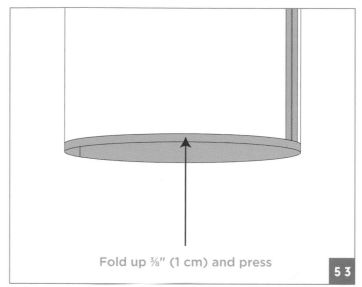

Fold up ⅜" (1 cm) and press

53

52. Close all the folds. Edgestitch around the perimeter of the Sash. Press.

FINISHING

53. Fold and press ⅜ inch (1 cm) of the bottom of the bodice or the Skirt Bottom Ruffle toward the wrong side.

54. Fold and press ½ inch (1.25 cm) toward the wrong side again.

55. Edgestitch close to the first fold.

56. Give the top or dress a good press and you are done!

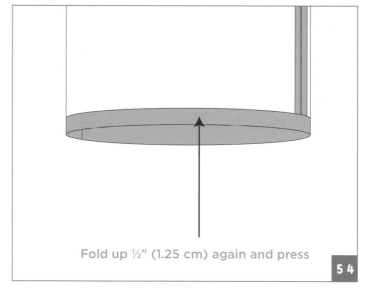

Fold up ½" (1.25 cm) again and press

54

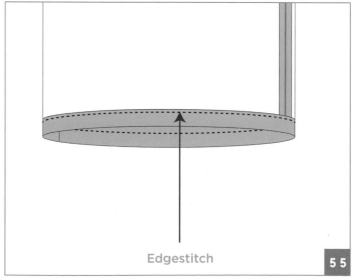

Edgestitch

55

THE OROSI

I am envious of people who can rock a high-waisted, babydoll-style knit top. I think it's cute and comfortable. You can go eat a Thanksgiving dinner and still look and feel chic afterward. However, the reality is that such a style is not always flattering for a pear-shaped person like me, and I don't think I am alone.

The Orosi is my resolution to this dilemma. It has the essence of a babydoll style but without the frumpiness. I made the peplum or skirt portion only slightly higher in the front, and the back waist is lower than the front. The transition from a higher front to a lower back is flattering while giving some visual interest. Your waist shaping is also more visible. All in all, it's a more pleasing look.

The Orosi has numerous features. It comes in a regular V neck with a neckband that overlaps at the center front. If you want something unique, there's an option to use a scarf collar. You can also make the Orosi into a top or dress with long or short sleeves. The top length hits slightly above the hip, while the dress length falls at the knees.

I have grouped the features into three views for simplicity, but you can definitely mix and match!

V-NECK TOP
(SEE PHOTO ON PAGE 4)

FRONT   BACK

V-NECK DRESS
(SEE PHOTO ON PAGE 6)

FRONT   BACK

SCARF-NECK TOP
(SEE PHOTO ON PAGE 130)

FRONT   BACK

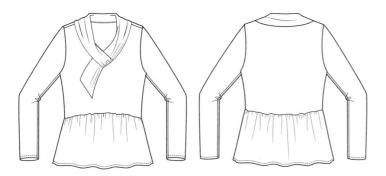

CHOOSING YOUR SIZE

1. Compare your bust circumference (the fullest part of your measured bust) to the "Body Measurements" table. Choose the size that best fits your bust. If your measurement is between sizes, choose the smaller size if you like your garment more fitted; otherwise, choose the bigger size.

2. Compare your waist circumference (the narrowest part of your measured waist) to the "Body Measurements" table. Choose the size that best fits your waist. If your measurement is between sizes, choose the smaller size if you like your garment more fitted; otherwise, choose the bigger size.

3. Compare your hip circumference (the fullest part of your measured hip) to the "Body Measurements" table. Choose the size that best fits your hips. If your measurement is between sizes, choose the smaller size if you like your garment more fitted; otherwise, choose the bigger size.

4. If you have different sizes for the bust, waist and hip, you can blend sizes (page 11).

MATERIALS

PRIMARY FABRIC

Use a very lightweight to medium-weight knit fabric with 65 to 85 percent horizontal stretch (page 10) and good recovery. Jersey, rayon spandex, double brushed polyester and cotton spandex are good choices.

OTHER MATERIALS

15 inches (38 cm) of ⅜-inch (1-cm)- or ½-inch (1.25-cm)-wide straight fusible stay tape (page 16); you can also cut your own using lightweight woven fusible interfacing on the straight grain.

⅜-inch (1-cm)- or ½-inch (1.25-cm)-wide clear elastic. For lengths, see the "Elastic Requirements" table on page 132.

BODY MEASUREMENTS

SIZE		00	0	2	4	6	8	10	12	14	16	18	20
BUST	(IN)	31⅛	32½	33⅞	35⅛	36½	37⅞	39¼	40⅝	42	43¼	44⅝	46
	(CM)	79	82.5	86	89	92.5	96	99.5	103	106.5	110	113.5	117
WAIST	(IN)	25⅜	26¾	28⅛	29½	30⅞	32¼	33⅝	35	36⅜	37¾	39⅛	40½
	(CM)	64.5	68	71.5	75	78.5	82	85.5	89	92.5	96	99.5	103
HIP	(IN)	33¼	34⅝	35⅞	37¼	38⅝	40	41¼	42⅝	44	45⅜	46⅝	48
	(CM)	84.5	88	91	94.5	98	101.5	105	108	112	115	118.5	122

FINISHED GARMENT MEASUREMENTS

SIZE		00	0	2	4	6	8	10	12	14	16	18	20
BUST	(IN)	29⅞	31⅜	32⅞	34⅜	35⅞	37⅜	38⅞	40⅜	41⅞	43⅜	44⅞	46⅜
	(CM)	76	80	83.5	87.5	91	95	99	102.5	106.5	110	114	118
WAIST	(IN)	26⅛	27⅝	29⅛	30⅝	32⅛	33½	35	36½	38	39½	41	42½
	(CM)	66	70	74	77.5	81.5	85	89	93	96.5	100.5	104.5	108
HIP	(IN)	48⅞	49⅞	50⅞	52	53	54⅛	55⅛	56⅛	57¼	58¼	59⅜	60⅜
	(CM)	124	126.5	129.5	132	134.5	137.5	140	142.5	145.5	148	150.5	153.5

FABRIC REQUIREMENTS

		00	0	2	4	6	8	10	12	14	16	18	20
PRIMARY FABRIC (54 INCHES/137 CM WIDE)													
V-NECK TOP	(YARD)	1	1	1	1½	1½	1½	1½	1½	1½	1½	1½	1½
	(CM)	90	90	90	135	135	135	135	135	135	135	135	135
V-NECK DRESS	(YARD)	1½	1½	1½	2⅛	2⅛	2⅛	2¼	2¼	2¼	2⅜	2⅜	2⅜
	(CM)	135	135	135	195	195	195	205	205	205	220	220	220
SCARF-NECK TOP	(YARD)	1⅞	1⅞	1⅞	1⅞	1⅞	1⅞	1⅞	1⅞	1⅞	2	2	2
	(CM)	170	170	170	170	170	170	170	170	170	180	180	180

ELASTIC REQUIREMENTS

	00	0	2	4	6	8	10	12	14	16	18	20
(INCH)	30⅝	32	33½	35	36⅜	37⅞	39⅜	40¾	42¼	43⅝	45⅛	46⅝
(CM)	77.5	81.5	85	89	92.5	96	100	103.5	107	111	114.5	118.5

FABRIC CUTTING INSTRUCTIONS

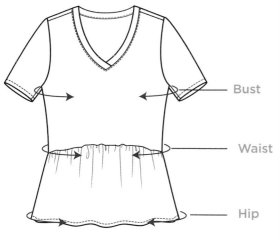

PATTERN PIECE	FROM PRIMARY FABRIC, CUT
1 - Top Front	1 on fold
2 - Top Back	1 on fold
3 - Bottom Front	1 on fold*
4 - Bottom Back	1 on fold*
5 - Sleeve	2 mirror images*
6 - Neckband (for V-Neck Top or V-Neck Dress only)	1 on fold
7 - Scarf Collar (for Scarf-Neck Top only)	1 on fold
*Use the hem line for V-Neck Top, V-Neck Dress or Scarf-Neck Top accordingly.	

Bust

Waist

Hip

LAYOUT DIAGRAMS
V-NECK TOP

SIZES 00 TO 2

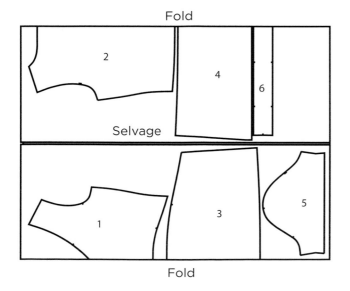

SIZES 4 TO 20

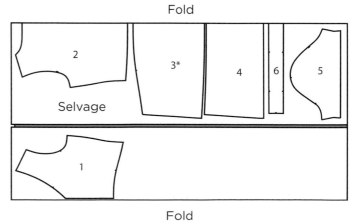

*Flip the pattern piece over to cut this piece

(CONTINUED)

LAYOUT DIAGRAMS

V-NECK DRESS

SIZES OO TO 2

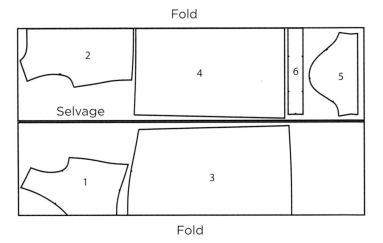

Fold

Selvage

Fold

SIZES 4 TO 20

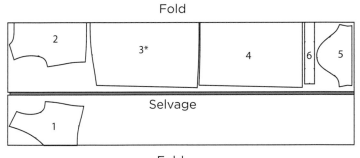

Fold

Selvage

Fold

*Flip the pattern piece over to cut this piece

SCARF-NECK TOP

SIZES OO TO 2

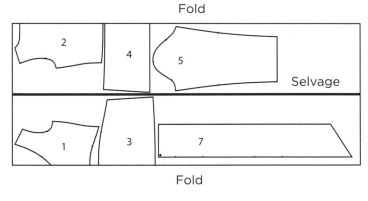

Fold

Selvage

Fold

SIZES 4 TO 20

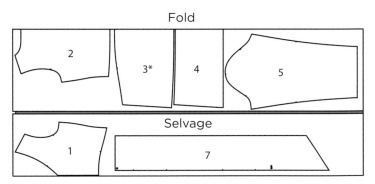

Fold

Selvage

Fold

*Flip the pattern piece over to cut this piece

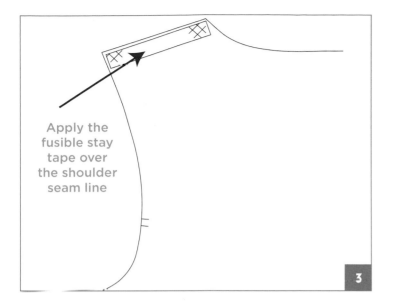

Apply the fusible stay tape over the shoulder seam line

3

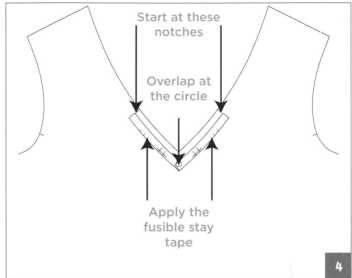

Start at these notches

Overlap at the circle

Apply the fusible stay tape

4

SEAM ALLOWANCES

The included seam allowances are ⅜ inch (1 cm) unless stated otherwise in the process.

PROCESS

CUTTING AND MARKING FABRIC

1. Trace the pattern outlines for your size and option onto a piece of paper (see back envelope), then cut the fabric according to the Layout Diagrams (pages 133–134).

2. Transfer all the markings to the fabric before removing the pattern pieces (pages 15–16).

STABILIZATION

3. Cut a length of fusible stay tape and, using a hot iron, apply onto the Top Back (2) shoulder on the wrong side, centered over the seam line. The seam line is ⅜ inch (1 cm) from the cut edge. Repeat for the other Top Back shoulder.

4. Cut two pieces of fusible stay tape and apply onto the neckline of the Top Front (1), starting from the lower notch to the point of the V, on both sides of the neckline, centered over the seam line. The seam line is ⅜ inch (1 cm) from the cut edge.

SHOULDER

5. With the right sides together, pin the Top Back to the Top Front at the shoulder. Stitch or serge. If you stitched the seam, press the seam allowances open and finish the seam allowances (page 18). If you serged the seam, press the seam allowances toward the Top Back. Repeat for the other shoulder.

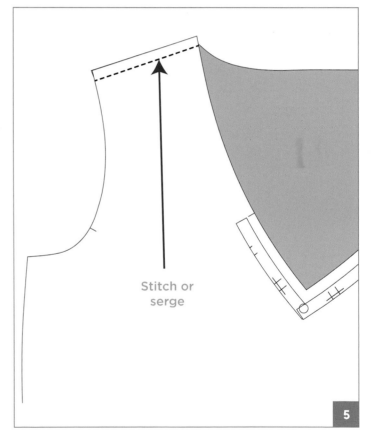

Stitch or serge

5

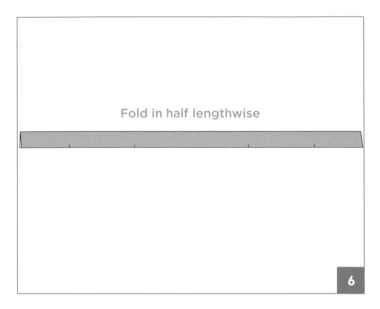

Fold in half lengthwise

6

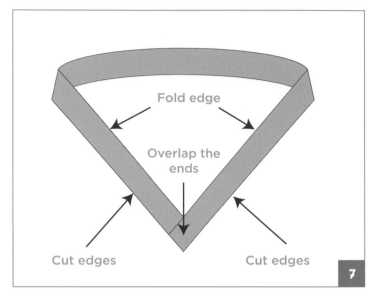

Fold edge

Overlap the ends

Cut edges   Cut edges

7

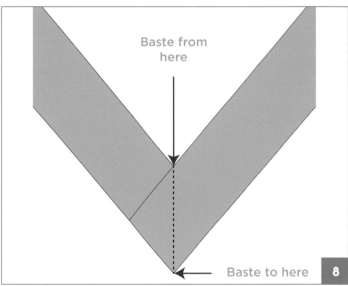

Baste from here

Baste to here   **8**

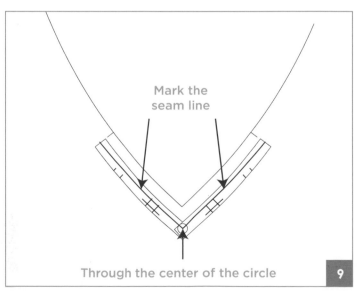

Mark the seam line

Through the center of the circle   **9**

NECKLINE

For the neckline of the V-Neck Top and V-Neck Dress, follow steps 6 to 18. For the Scarf-Neck Top's scarf collar, skip to step 19.

6. With the right side inside, fold and press the Neckband (6) in half lengthwise.

7. Overlap the ends of the folded Neckband to form a V shape. The folded edge should be at the inside, and the cut edges should be at the outside. If you put the left over right, then the finished Neckband will be right over left and vice versa. But either way will work.

8. Baste (page 17) the layers together in a straight line from the upper point of the V to the lower point of the V.

9. On the Top Front, starting at the lower notch on one side of the V neck, using an erasable marker or chalk, mark the ⅜-inch (1-cm) seam line to the center of the circle, then mark from the center of the circle up to the notch on the other side of the V neck.

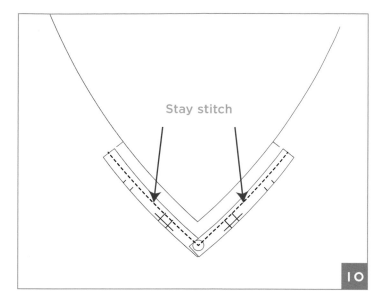

Stay stitch

`10`

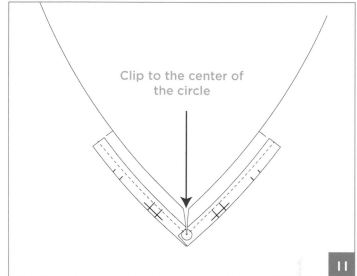

Clip to the center of the circle

`11`

10. Stay stitch (page 20) exactly on the V as you marked in the previous step, pivoting at the point of the V (the center of the circle).

11. Using your scissors, clip to, but not beyond, the stitch line at the point of the V.

12. With the Top Front right side up, pin the center seam of the Neckband to the neckline, with the point of the Neckband aligning with the point of the V on the neckline (not the bottom of the clip that you made). Be sure that the basting stitch on the Neckband is vertical.

13. Pull one side of the Front V neck downward so you are spreading open the clip of the Front until one side of the neckline aligns with one side of the Neckband, matching notches and cut edges.

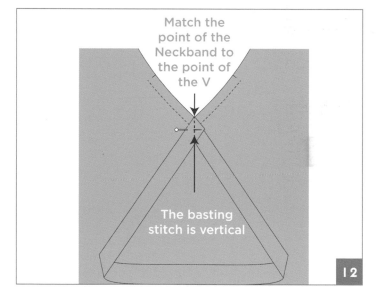

Match the point of the Neckband to the point of the V

The basting stitch is vertical

`12`

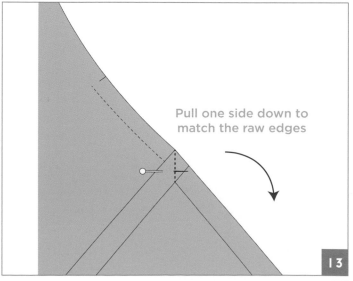

Pull one side down to match the raw edges

`13`

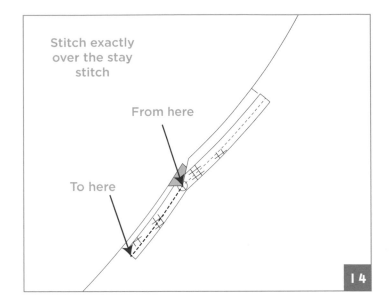

Stitch exactly
over the stay
stitch

From here

To here

14

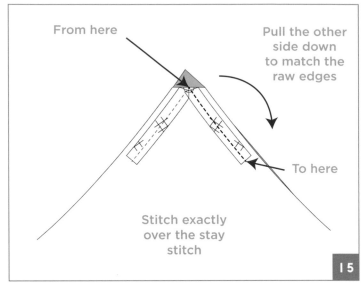

From here

Pull the other
side down
to match the
raw edges

To here

Stitch exactly
over the stay
stitch

15

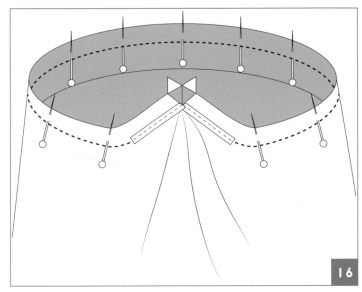

16

14. Turn over to the wrong side so you can see the stay stitching; stitch exactly over the stay stitch on one side of the V through all layers.

15. Align the other side of the neckline with the Neckband, with the cut edges even. From the wrong side of the Front, where the line of stay stitch is visible, stitch exactly over the stay stitch on the remaining side of the V through all layers.

16. Stretch to pin the rest of the Neckband along the neckline of the Top Front and Top Back, matching the lower notches, notches on the Neckband to the shoulder seams and center back to center back. Note that you will need to stretch the Neckband more on the back portion than the front portion.

17. Stitch around the neckline through all layers; be sure to connect with the V previously stitched. Press the seam allowances toward the Top Front and Top Back. Finish the neckline seam.

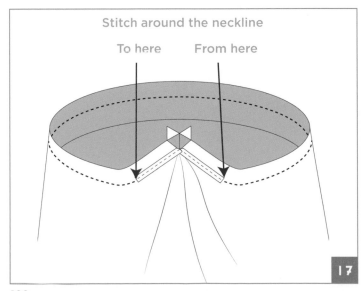

Stitch around the neckline

To here   From here

17

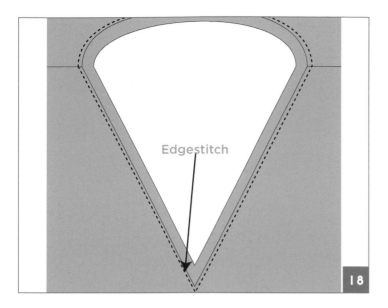

Edgestitch

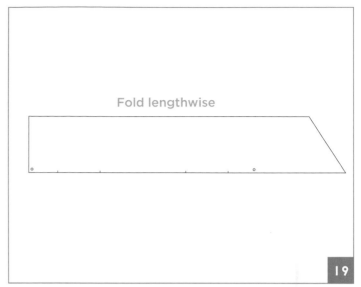

Fold lengthwise

18. From the right side, edgestitch (page 20) next to the neckband on the Top Front and Top Back through the seam allowances underneath, starting from the center back, around to the point of the V and ending at the center back. Remove the baste stitching at the center front of the Neckband. Press.

SCARF COLLAR

Follow steps 19 to 41 for the Scarf-Neck Top's scarf collar.

19. With the right side inside, fold the Scarf Collar (7) in half lengthwise.

20. Pin the cut edges together, matching the circles, triangles and notches.

21. On the short flat end, stitch from the edge to the triangle. Stitch back and forth at the triangle to secure the end of the stitch line.

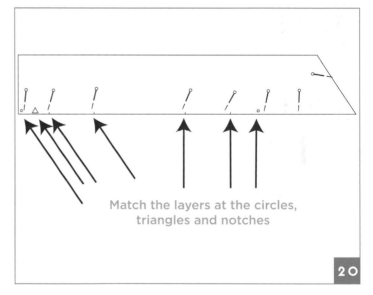

Match the layers at the circles, triangles and notches

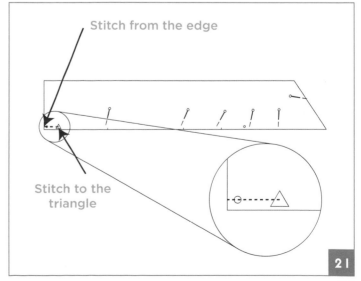

Stitch from the edge

Stitch to the triangle

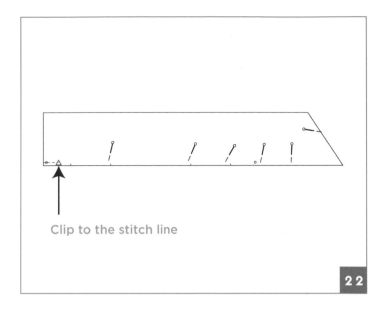

Clip to the stitch line

22

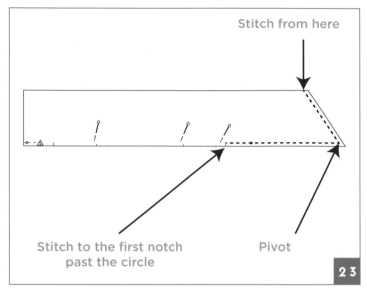

Stitch from here

Stitch to the first notch
past the circle

Pivot

23

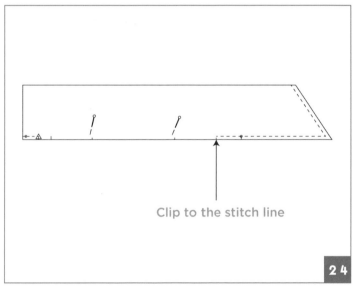

Clip to the stitch line

24

22. Using your scissors, clip from the edge to the end of the stitch line.

23. Stitch the slanted short end of the Scarf Collar from the fold toward the pointy end of the Scarf Collar. Pivot the stitch line so you can continue to stitch along the edge. Stitch past the circle marked CF, then stop at the first notch past the circle. Stitch back and forth to secure the end of the stitch line.

24. Using your scissors, clip from the edge to the end of the stitch line.

25. Trim the seam allowances to ⅛ inch (3 mm)— however, only trim the seam allowances next to the sewn seam, not the unsewn portion.

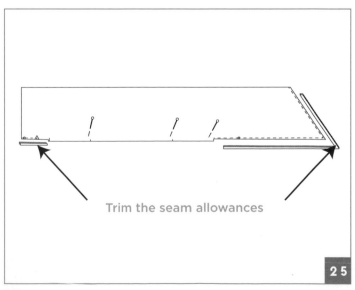

Trim the seam allowances

25

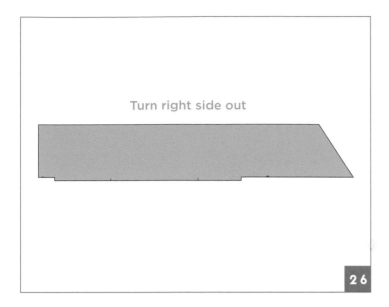

Turn right side out

26

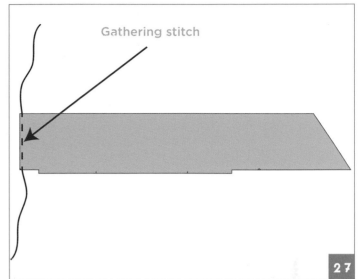

Gathering stitch

27

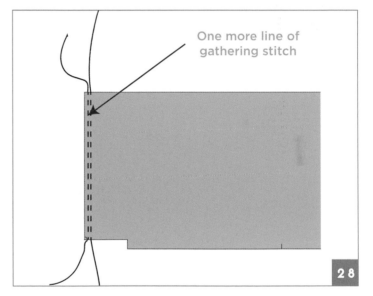

One more line of
gathering stitch

28

26. Turn the Scarf Collar right side out and press.

27. Using a long stitch length of 4 mm, stitch along the flat short end through both layers, leaving long tails of thread at the beginning and the end. This stitch line is ¼ inch (6 mm) from the cut edge. This line of stitching is referred to as gathering stitch.

28. Stitch another line of gathering stitch using a long stitch length (4 mm) between the first one and the cut edge, but take care not to stitch over the first stitch line.

29. On the Top Front, starting at the lower notch on one side of the V neck, mark the ⅜-inch (1-cm) seam line to the center of the circle, then mark from the center of the circle up to the notch on the other side of the V neck.

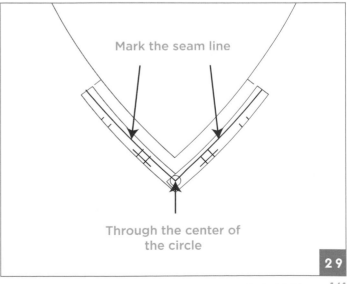

Mark the seam line

Through the center of
the circle

29

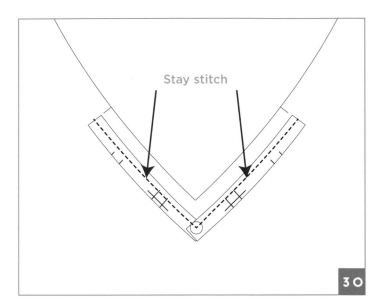

Stay stitch

30

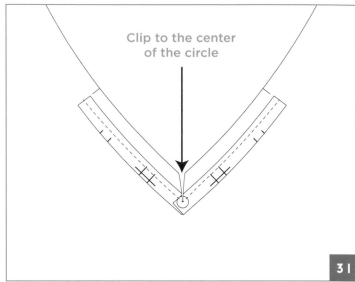

Clip to the center of the circle

31

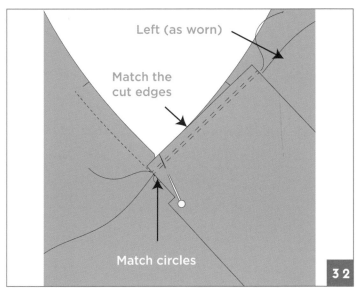

Left (as worn)

Match the cut edges

Match circles

32

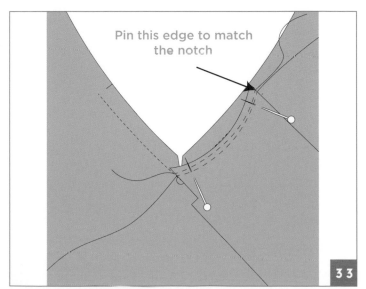

Pin this edge to match the notch

33

30. Stay stitch exactly on the V as you marked in the previous step, pivoting at the point of the V (the center of the circle).

31. Using your scissors, clip to, but not beyond, the stitch line at the point of the V.

32. Pin the short flat end of the Scarf Collar to the right side of the Top Front on the left (as worn), matching the center of the circle on the Scarf Collar (on the short flat end) to the center of the circle of the Top Front, as well as the cut edges.

33. Pin the other sewn edge of the Scarf Collar to the notch on the Top Front.

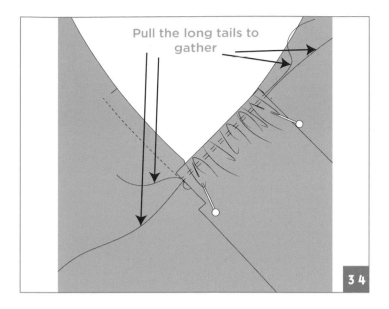

Pull the long tails to gather

34

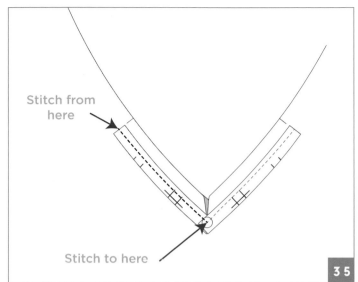

Stitch from here

Stitch to here

35

34. Pull the long tails of the stitch line to gather the short flat end of the Scarf Collar so that the length matches the length on the neckline. The cut edges of all layers should be aligned.

35. Turn over to the wrong side so you can see the stay stitching; stitch exactly over the stay stitch on the left side (as worn) of the V through all layers.

36. From the right side, pull the right neckline (as worn) down until the triangle on the neckline matches the clip (the triangle) on the Scarf Collar. Pin.

37. Rearrange the neckline so that both sides are up. Note that in order for the Scarf Collar to remain flat and not twisted, the center front is not at the bottom of the V neck anymore.

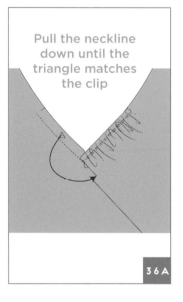

Pull the neckline down until the triangle matches the clip

36A

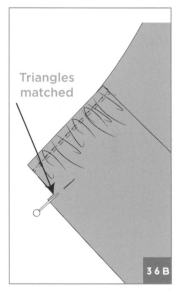

Triangles matched

36B

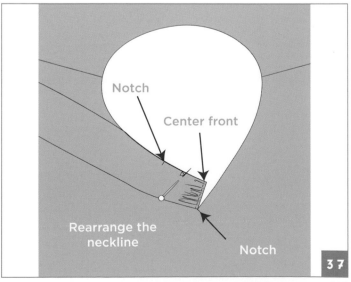

Notch

Center front

Rearrange the neckline

Notch

37

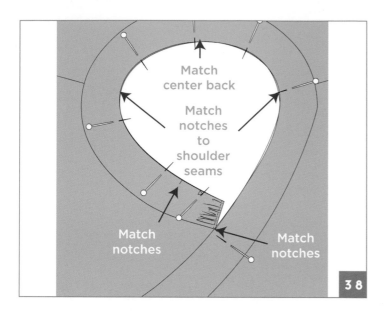

Match
center back

Match
notches
to
shoulder
seams

Match
notches

Match
notches

38

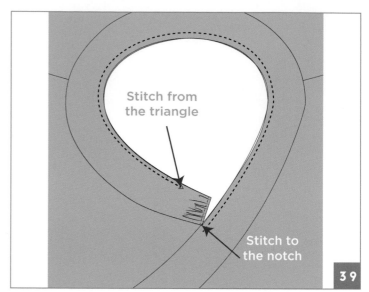

Stitch from
the triangle

Stitch to
the notch

39

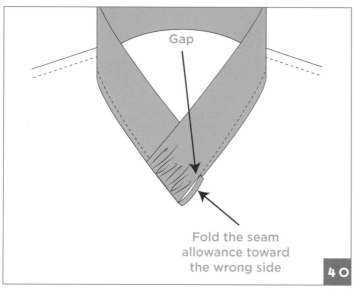

Gap

Fold the seam
allowance toward
the wrong side

40

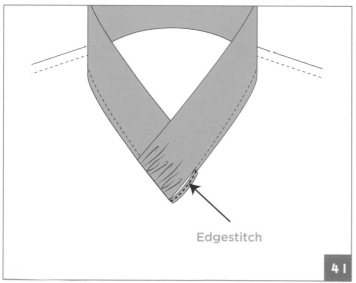

Edgestitch

41

38. Continue to pin the rest of the Scarf Collar to the neckline, matching the notches, notch to shoulder seam, center backs, notch to shoulder seam and notches. Note that the free hanging side of the Scarf Collar comes down on the left side (as worn). Be sure not to twist the Scarf Collar.

39. Stitch the Scarf Collar to the neckline, but do not stitch the portion where the Scarf Collar is already sewn. In other words, stitch from the triangle of the Top Front, through the back neckline to the notch of the Top Front. Press the seam allowances toward the Top Front and Top Back. Finish the seam allowances of the entire neckline.

40. On the right-hand side of the Top Front (as worn) where there is an opening, fold the seam allowance toward the wrong side.

41. With the Scarf Collar out of the way, edgestitch next to the fold.

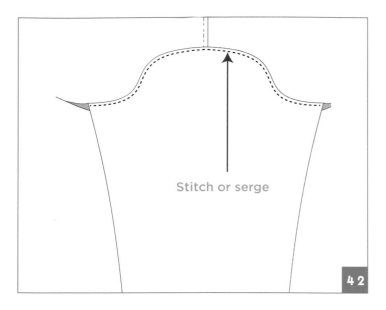

Stitch or serge

42

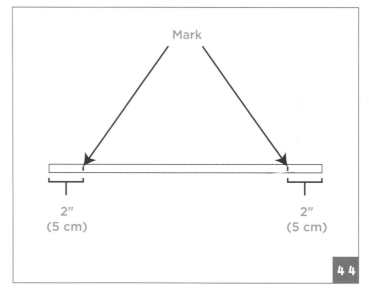

Sleeve seam

Side seam

Stitch or serge

43

SLEEVES

42. With the right sides together, pin the Sleeve (5) to the Top Front and Top Back, matching single notch to single notch, sleeve cap notch to shoulder seam and double notch to double notch. Stitch or serge. Press the seam allowances toward the Sleeve. Finish the seam allowances if you stitched the seam. Repeat for the other Sleeve.

SIDE

43. With the right sides together, pin the Top Front to the Top Back, matching notches and underarm seams. Stitch or serge from the bottom edge of the bodice to the bottom edge of the Sleeve. If you stitched the seam, press the seam allowances open and finish the seam allowances. If you serged the seam, press it toward the Top Back. Repeat for the other side.

PEPLUM OR SKIRT

44. Using a pen, mark 2 inches (5 cm) from the beginning and from the end of the clear elastic. The beginning and end sections are for holding onto while working with the clear elastic.

45. This step and the next two steps are to divide the middle section into eight parts of equal length. To do so, fold the clear elastic in half with the cut edges even. Using a pen, mark the opposite folded end. This is the midpoint of the elastic. Note that the marks made in the previous step are brought together as well; we will refer to them together as H.

Mark

2"
(5 cm)

2"
(5 cm)

44

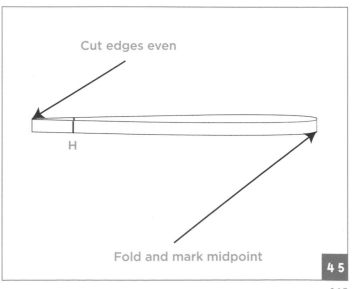

Cut edges even

H

Fold and mark midpoint

45

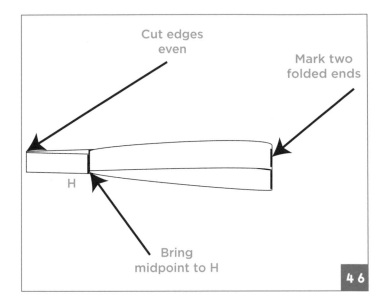

Cut edges even

Mark two folded ends

H

Bring midpoint to H

46

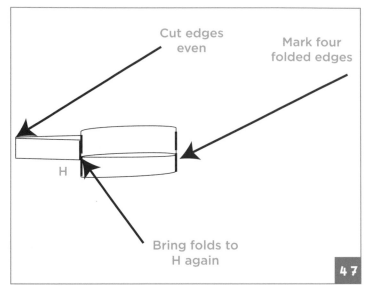

Cut edges even

Mark four folded edges

H

Bring folds to H again

47

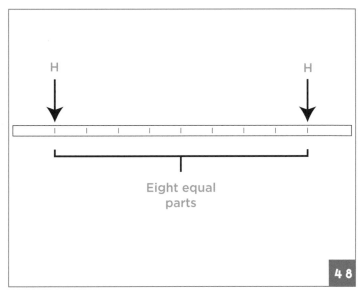

H   H

Eight equal parts

48

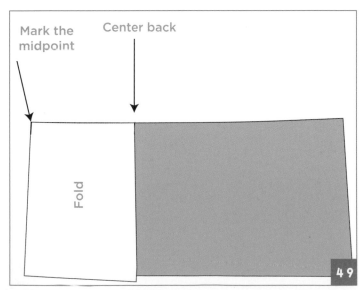

Mark the midpoint

Center back

Fold

49

46. Fold the clear elastic again and bring the midpoint of the elastic to H. Using a pen, mark the opposite folded ends. The middle section of the clear elastic has now been divided into four parts.

47. Repeat one more time by bringing the folds to H. Using a pen, mark the opposite folded ends.

48. The middle section, excluding the 2-inch (5-cm) sections on each end, now has been divided into eight parts.

49. On the Bottom Back (4), you should already have a mark of the center back (see Center Fold, page 15), which is where the fabric was cut on the fold. Bring the side edge to meet the center back, and the resulting fold is the midpoint between the center back and the side. Using an erasable marker or chalk, mark the midpoint. You only need to mark at the top of the Bottom Back (the slightly curved edge without a notch). Repeat for the other side.

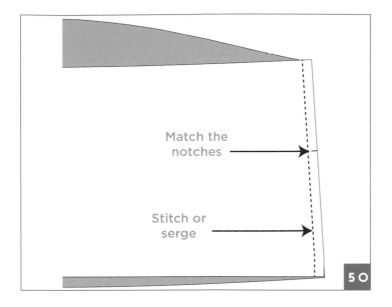

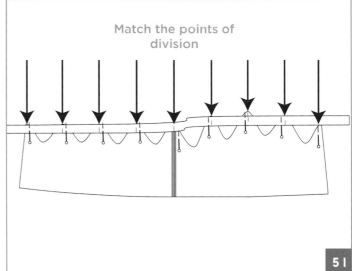

50. With the right sides together, pin the Bottom Back to the Bottom Front (3) at one side, matching the notches. Stitch or serge. If you stitched the seam, press the seam allowances open and finish the seam allowances. If you serged the seam, press it toward the Bottom Front. Do not stitch or serge the other side yet; it will be sewn in a later step. This assembled Bottom Back and Bottom Front will now be referred to as the Skirt.

51. With the marks, notches and seam, the top edge of the Skirt is already divided into eight portions. Pin the clear elastic onto the wrong side of the skirt, aligning the points of division as well as the top edge. There should be 2 inches (5 cm) of extra clear elastic protruding from each end. Note that the elastic is shorter in length than the Skirt.

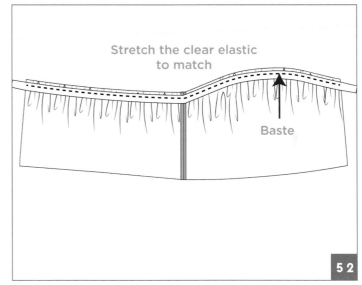

52. Baste the clear elastic onto the top of the Skirt while stretching the clear elastic. To safely baste the elastic, take a few stitches without stretching. Then stretch by pulling the extra clear elastic behind the presser foot as well as the clear elastic and fabric in the front of the presser foot. Take a few more stitches while stretching. Always use both hands to stretch so you don't strain the needle. You will only be able to stitch one or two inches or a few centimeters at a time. Anchor the needle in the fabric to readjust, and repeat the process of stretching while stitching until you get to the end. As the clear elastic stretches back, the assembled Bottom Front and Bottom Back is gathered as a result.

53. Trim the extra clear elastic at the beginning and end.

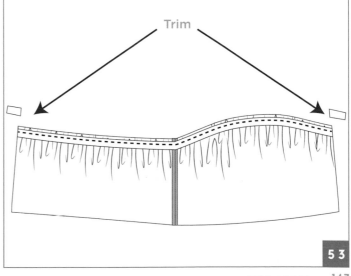

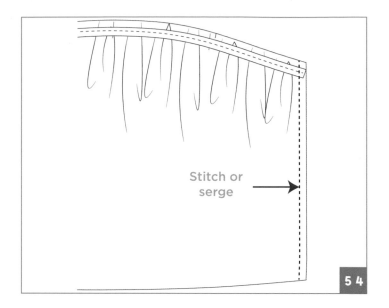

Stitch or serge

54

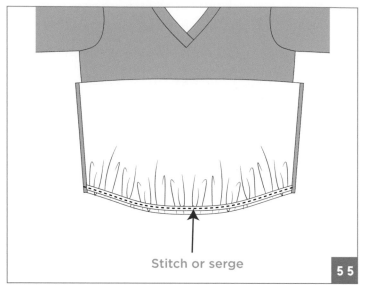

Stitch or serge

55

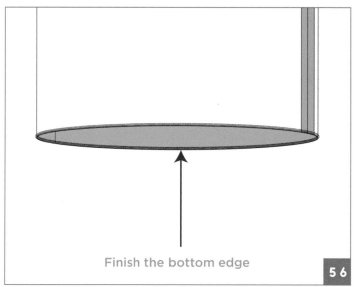

Finish the bottom edge

56

54. With the right sides together, pin the Bottom Back to the Bottom Front at the other side. Stitch or serge. If you stitched the seam, press the seam allowances open and finish the seam allowances. If you serged the seam, press it toward the Bottom Back.

FINISHING

55. With the right sides together, pin the gathered edge of the assembled Bottom Front and Bottom Back to the bottom of the assembled Top Front and Top Back, matching center front and center back, notches and side seams. Stitch or serge. Press the seam allowances toward the top. Finish the seam allowances.

56. Finish the bottom cut edge of the skirt.

57. Fold and press ¾ inch (1.9 cm) toward the wrong side.

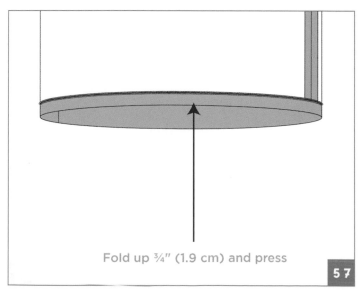

Fold up ¾″ (1.9 cm) and press

57

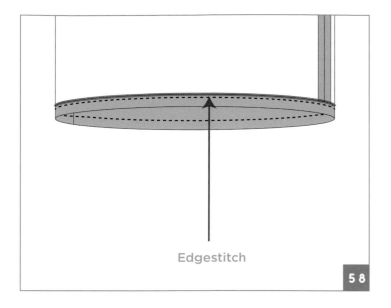

Edgestitch

58

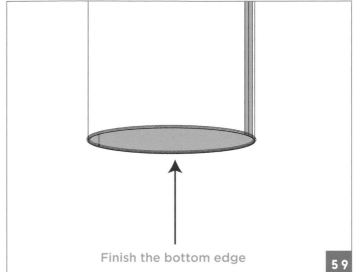

Finish the bottom edge

59

58. Edgestitch close to the cut edge.

59. Finish the bottom cut edge of the Sleeve.

60. Fold and press ¾ inch (1.9 cm) toward the wrong side.

61. Edgestitch close to the cut edge.

62. Give the top or dress a good press and you are done! If you made the Scarf-Neck Top, tuck the scarf portion through the opening when wearing.

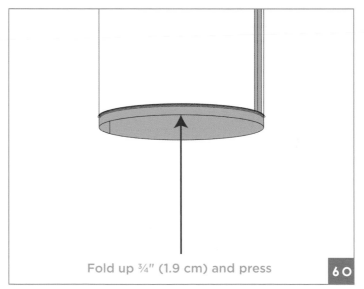

Fold up ¾" (1.9 cm) and press

60

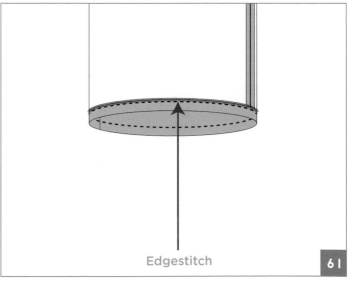

Edgestitch

61

THANK YOU!

Even though my name is on the front cover, this book really was a team effort.

The man behind the photos in *Sew Beautiful* is my husband, Ray Morgan, but he wore many more hats than just being the cameraman. Honey, thank you for putting up with me. Thank you for not asking "Are we done yet?" when taking a million photos. Thank you for your patience when I constantly interrupted you by asking "Do you like this sentence?" or "Does this top go with this skirt?" Even though you don't care about the difference between purple and magenta, I know you care a whole lot about my happiness. You do everything to support me and contribute to my success. You make me feel like life is full of possibilities and adventure. I am proud to have you as my husband. I love you so much. We are a team.

I feel so fortunate to be surrounded by amazing people from the sewing community who supported and encouraged me. These talented women helped me test the patterns in this book so that I could deliver a high-quality product to our readers: Aimee Wilson, Andrea Clark, Angela Hougardy, Anita Holgate, Annick Campenaerts, Bernice van der Meer, Brooke Church, Carmen Statham, Cass Hausserman, Chiara Kruse, Christiane Siemon, Christine Griffin Grace, Crystal Kashuba, Denise Keierleber, Diana Roberson, Diane Cullum, Elsa Pomar, Erika Janik, Ilse Lemmens, Indu Ankareddi, Jackie Burney, Jan Murry, Jen Ballif, Jenny Bowen, Jodi Christopher Williams, Jolien Thissen, Jordan Anderson, Judy O'Day, Kadri Kivistik, Karen Turner, Karina Trinidad, Katie Kennedy, Kayla Smith, Kelle Lujan, Kelsey Cushing, Kyema Greeley, Leanne Miller, Lim Boon Kuan, Linda Portsch, Lone Thomsen, Lorene Voskinarian, Margaret Winters, Maria Navarro Girbes, Melissa Ouellette, Michele Matsumoto, Natasha Tung, Nicole Golsteijn-Cnoops, Pam Black, Renata Harris, Sarah Hoggett, Sarah Jane Locke, Sharon Madsen, Stacey Clements, Taryn Haynes-Smart, Tiina Kirsipuu, Whitney Luckenbil and Yolanda Cuenca.

Let me give special thanks to Crystal Rice and Rita Parenteau. Not only did you test and proofread the patterns, but you were also my trusty sounding boards. I appreciate your friendship!

My sincere thanks go to Emily Taylor, my editor. This book would not exist if you didn't take a chance on me. Thank you, Emily! Meg Baskis, Laura Benton and the design team did a fantastic job on the creatives of the book. Thank you so much! Last but never least, I am so grateful for my publisher, Page Street Publishing Co. You made this book a reality and made my dream come true!

ABOUT THE AUTHOR

Kennis Wong is the founder and designer of Itch to Stitch Designs, an independent sewing pattern company specializing in high-quality digital sewing patterns for hobbyists. Kennis's sewing patterns have been featured in *Threads*, *Sew News*, *Love Sewing* and *Sew*.

itch-to-stitch.com
Instagram @itchtostitch
Facebook.com/groups/ItchToStitchDesigns

INDEX